SOUTH-WESTERN

PAGEMAKER® 5.0
FOR WINDOWS® AND MACINTOSH®

· ·

QuickTorial™

William R. Pasewark, Sr.
PROFESSOR EMERITUS, TEXAS TECH UNIVERSITY
OFFICE MANAGEMENT CONSULTANT

SOUTH-WESTERN EDUCATIONAL PUBLISHING

I(T)P™
International Thomson Publishing

South-Western Educational Publishing is a division of International
Thomson Publishing, Inc. The ITP trademark is used under license.

ISBN: 0-538-71505-7
1 2 3 4 5 6 7 8 PR 3 2 1 0 9 8 7 6
Printed in the United States of America

Editor in Chief: Robert E. First
Managing Editor: Janie Schwark
Developmental Editor: Dave Lafferty
Consulting Editor/Production Coordinator: Jane Congdon
Technical Editor: Rose Corgan
Fee Writer: Susan E. L. Lake
Marketing Manager: Kent Christensen
Senior Quality Assurance Specialist: Michael Jackson
Production: Custom Editorial Productions, Inc.

PageMaker is a trademark of Adobe Systems Incorporated.

Preface

TO THE STUDENT

PageMaker 5.0 for Windows and Macintosh is a desktop publishing program because it combines text and graphics using a computer to create an attractive and stimulating publication. This program can be used to produce newsletters, letterheads, business cards, and invitations. Desktop publishing software is used in personal, academic, career, and business settings to produce publications quickly and professionally.

The author planned this book to provide a realistic, complete, and successful learning experience for you. Objectives listed at the beginning of each lesson give you an overview of the lesson. Short segments of text explain new information and tell why it is important. Then, numbered steps help guide you through the computer operation exercises. These exercises give you a chance to practice the concepts you have just learned. The book includes many illustrations and exercises to simplify complex concepts and operations. Activity questions and review exercises help you review the lessons.

STUDENT'S GUIDE FOR USING THIS BOOK

The following terminology and procedures are used in this book:

- *Text* means words, numbers, and symbols that are printed.

- *Keying* means entering text into a computer. The terms *keying* and *typing* are sometimes used interchangeably.

- To save time and reduce the possibility of making errors, key the commands and filenames in lower case. In Windows, the program automatically converts them to upper case (capital) letters.

The different type styles used in this book have special meanings:

- Text that you will key into the computer is in bold type.

  Example: Key in the following words: **Place your name in the blank.**

- File names are bold and in all capital letters.

  Example: **EX5-4**

- Directory names are in italics and in all capital letters.

  Example: *LAYOUT*

- Words in the book that you will also see on the screen are in italics.

  Example: *tomorrow*

- Actions you are to take will be in bold.

  Example: Press **Enter.**

- The + sign between commands means to hold down the first key, press the second key, and release the two keys simultaneously. But, do not hold down the + key.

  Example: Shift + Tab

 ## TO THE TEACHER

Students enter computer courses with widely varying levels of skill and knowledge. Some may already know several software programs; others may have limited computer experience. *PageMaker 5.0 for Windows and Macintosh: QuickTorial™* is designed to help all students develop computer competency using a desktop publishing program.

This book has been structured to encourage a mastery level of learning. It follows the Madeline Hunter model which consists of input, modeling, guided practice, and independent practice before final check for mastery is completed. Exercises can be treated as guided practice and reviews as independent practice. Activities check for the students' understanding of content.

Average completion time for the book is 12–15 hours but will vary depending on the student's ability and previous computer experience. This book is appropriate for students in a variety of educational settings, including high schools, community colleges, continuing education programs, vocational-technical schools, career colleges, weekend courses, adult education programs, and personal instruction. The reading level and instructional pattern make it appropriate for a wide variety of learners, from youths to senior adults.

 ## SYSTEM REQUIREMENTS

Windows

- 486- or 386- based DOS-compatible computer
- Microsoft Windows 3.1 (or later)
- 4 MB of RAM memory
- 40 MB hard drive

- a high-resolution graphics adapter card (such as Super VGA or XGA)
- a mouse

Macintosh
- Apple Macintosh II series, Quadra, or SE/30 Computer
- System 7.0 or later
- 5 MB of RAM memory
- 80 MB hard drive

▶ INSTRUCTIONAL PACKAGE

The instructional package includes the student's book, template disks, solutions disks, and Teacher's Manual.

The ***student's book*** is organized around the following features:

- ***Objectives*** at the beginning of each lesson give students an overview of the lesson.
- ***Concepts*** are explained in short, easy-to-understand segments with illustrations to serve as reference points.
- ***Exercises*** immediately follow the presentation of new concepts. The instructions give students the opportunity to practice what they have just learned.
- ***Activity questions*** test for students' knowledge of concepts.
- ***Review Exercises*** check the students' understanding of the concepts and operations.
- A ***comprehensive index*** provides quick and easy accessibility to specific parts of the book.

Template disks contain pre-keyed text and selected graphics for Exercises and Review Exercises and may be copied for students. These disks allow students to use class time learning desktop publishing, rather than keying lengthy text into the computer.

Solutions disks contain solutions to Exercises and Review Exercises so that you can check students' work.

The ***Teacher's Manual*** includes the following features to ensure a successful and an enjoyable teaching experience:

- ***General teaching suggestions*** that are strategies for effective instruction with a minimum of stress.
- ***Specific teaching suggestions*** for each lesson.
- An ***answer key*** for activities.
- ***Solutions*** for Exercises and Review Exercises.

ACKNOWLEDGMENTS

I thank Susan Lake, a teacher at Lubbock-Cooper High School; Jane Congdon, a Consulting Editor at South-Western Educational Publishing; and Dawna Walls, a professional technical writer who worked diligently, cooperatively, and rapidly to produce this book. I also thank Stephen Collings, a student at Lubbock High School, who keystroke-edited the book. Their work will help our teachers to teach better and our students to learn about an exciting desktop publishing program—PageMaker 5.0.

Many professional South-Western sales representatives make educationally sound presentations to teachers about our books. I have traveled with them "on the road," so I know first-hand and appreciate very much their valuable function as "bridges" between the author and teacher.

William R. Pasewark, Sr.

BOOKS BY THE AUTHORS

The Pasewark books listed here are available exclusively from South-Western Educational Publishing.

Tutorial and Applications Series

ClarisWorks 4.0 for Macintosh

Microsoft Works for Windows 2.0: Tutorial and Applications (for high school)

Microsoft Works for Windows 2.0: A Practical Approach (for college)

Microsoft Works for Windows 3.0

Microsoft Works 4.0 for Windows 95

Microsoft Office 7.0 for Windows 95

Express Publisher 3.0

PFS: First Publisher

Publish It! IBM and Apple

QuickTorial™ Series

Microsoft Works for Windows 3.0 (Quick Course)

Microsoft Works 4.0 for Windows 95

Microsoft Office for Windows 95

PageMaker 5.0

PageMaker 6.0

Applications for Reinforcement Series

Microsoft Works 2.0/3.0 for Windows

Microsoft Works 4.0 for Windows 95

Table of Contents

LESSON 1

PageMaker Introduction

OBJECTIVES

After completing this lesson, you will be able to:

1. Start PageMaker.
2. Create a new publication.
3. Identify parts of the publication window.
4. Open an existing publication.
5. Print a publication.
6. Save a publication.
7. Close a publication.
8. End a PageMaker session.

Estimated Time: 1 hour

INTRODUCTION

PageMaker is the world's best-selling desktop-publishing program. It gives you the power to create professional-looking publications such as brochures, newsletters, and reports. PageMaker is available in two versions: one for the Macintosh and one for Windows-based computers. When instructions are different, they are labeled *Windows* and *Macintosh*.

STARTING PAGEMAKER

PageMaker is started from the Program Manager in Windows and the desktop in Macintosh.

> To start PageMaker:

Windows

* Double-click the **Aldus** icon.

Macintosh

* Double-click the **Aldus** folder in Macintosh.
* Double-click the **PageMaker 5.0 icon.**

N O T E

Pressing and then quickly releasing the mouse button is called clicking. Clicking twice rapidly is called double-clicking.

CREATING A NEW PUBLICATION

When you start PageMaker, an empty page appears on the screen. You must use the menu at the top of the page to create a new publication.

> To access a menu:

Windows

* Point to the menu name and click. A menu will drop down from the name, displaying the choices available.
* Click the command you want to use.

Macintosh

* Point to the menu name and press and hold down the mouse button. A menu will drop down from the name, displaying the choices available.
* Drag the cursor down the menu and release the mouse button on the command you want to use.

> To create a new publication using the default settings:

* Choose **New** from the **File** menu. The Page setup dialog box appears as shown in Figure 1–1.
* Choose **OK** to accept the default settings. An empty page appears on the pasteboard, as shown in Figure 1–2.

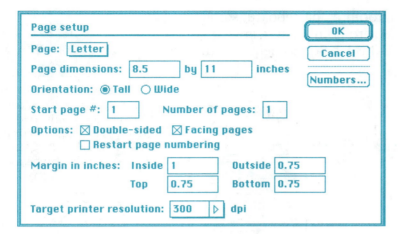

Figure 1-1
The Page setup dialog box offers a variety of page options that will be used in creating future publications.

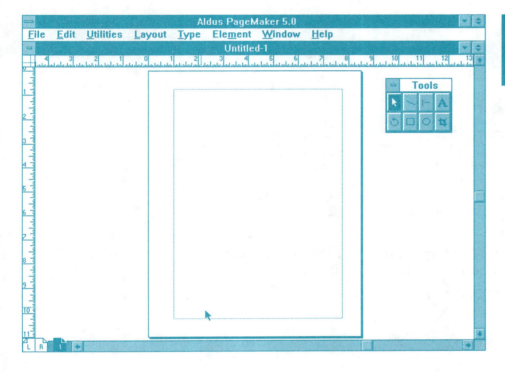
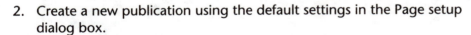
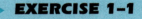

Figure 1-2
After you choose the default settings, a blank page is displayed on the pasteboard.

1. Start PageMaker. An empty page is shown on the screen.

2. Create a new publication using the default settings in the Page setup dialog box.

3. Leave the publication open for the next exercise.

EXERCISE 1-1

VIEWING THE PUBLICATION WINDOW

The blank page shown in Figure 1-3 is called a publication window. The margins of the page are shown with a dotted line. The other parts of the publication window are the close box, menu bar, title bar, vertical and horizontal rulers, toolbox, pasteboard, scroll bars, page icons, master page icons, and zero point. These are explained in the following sections. Figure 1–3 is labeled to help identify each part.

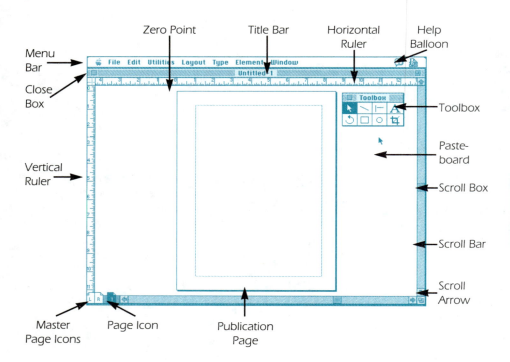

Notice the Help balloon or menu on the menu bar. Pulling it down will reveal ways to access information about various PageMaker features. Use it whenever you need additional instruction.

Figure 1–3
In the publication window, menu bars, tool boxes, and scroll bars give you control of your publication.

The Close Box

The close box in the upper-left corner allows you to close the window. Closing makes the window disappear from the screen.

To close a PageMaker publication:

Windows

• Double-click on the close box.

Macintosh

• Click on the close box.

The Menu Bar

The menu bar lists the names of the currently available menus.

Zero Point

The zero point is the point on your page where the zeros on the horizontal and vertical rulers meet. When you start a new publication, the zero point is at the upper-left corner of the page. You can move the zero point anywhere along the ruler by dragging it to a new location.

When you pull down a menu, notice the symbols to the right of some menu selections. These are keyboard shortcuts. They can be used instead of pulling down the menu by using either the control key (Windows) or the command key (Macintosh) plus a letter.

Horizontal Ruler

The horizontal ruler located at the top of the screen helps you align text and graphics to specific measurements. The unit of measure shown is inches, but you can change it to picas using the Preferences command.

Title Bar

The title bar shows the name of the window. In most cases, this will be the name of the publication you are viewing in the window.

Toolbox

The toolbox, shown in Figure 1–4, contains tools you will use to create, edit, and move text and graphics. Table 1–1 lists the tools and their functions.

To select a tool:

- Point to the tool and click.

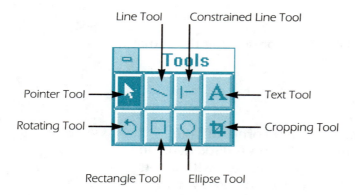

Figure 1–4
The toolbox provides tools for manipulating text and graphics.

■ Table 1–1

Tool	Function
Pointer tool	Selects and moves text and graphics
Line tool	Draws straight lines
Constrained line tool	Draws straight lines at 45-degree angles
Text tool	Selects and keys text
Cropping tool	Crops imported graphics
Ellipse tool	Draws ovals and circles
Rectangle tool	Draws rectangles and squares
Rotating tool	Rotates text blocks and graphics

Pasteboard

The pasteboard is the empty space around the page on the screen. You can place text and graphics in this area and move them onto your page later.

Scroll Bars, Boxes, and Arrows

When a file contains more information than the window can display, scroll bars appear. Scroll arrows and scroll boxes are located within scroll bars and are used to move the page vertically or horizontally. The scroll boxes indicate your approximate position in the publication.

Clicking on the scroll arrows moves the page a short distance. Click above or below the scroll box to move longer distances. You can also drag the scroll box to move quickly to a specific part of a page.

Scroll bars appear in places other than publication windows. In the Open dialog box, you will see scroll bars on the Files and Directories boxes.

Publication Page

The publication page shows a solid outline representing the actual page. Dotted lines indicate text margins.

Page Icons

Numbered page icons appear in the lower-left corner of your screen. The icon for the page you are working on is darkened. On your screen, only one page is shown, and it is marked with a 1. If you added another page, you would see an icon marked with a 2 for the second page. You will learn how to insert pages in another lesson. To move to a certain page in a PageMaker publication, click on the appropriate numbered page icon.

Master Page Icons

The master page icons are to the left of the numbered page icons. The page marked with an L is for the left master page and the page with the R is for the right master page. The master pages contain formatting data for all the pages in your publication, but they do not print.

Vertical Ruler

The vertical ruler at the left side of the screen helps you align text and graphics to specific measurements. The unit of measure shown is inches, but you can change it to picas using the Preferences command.

1. Practice pulling down menus.

2. Practice moving the publication vertically and horizontally using the arrows and the scroll boxes.

3. Choose **Close** from the **File** menu. If a dialog box appears, asking if you wish to save changes, click **No.** The blank page disappears.

4. Leave the empty publication window open for the next exercise.

EXERCISE 1–2

OPENING AN EXISTING PUBLICATION

You can open publications from any drive or directory. The Open publication dialog box, as shown in Figure 1–5, enables you to open a file from any available disk and directory. Directories can contain files, as well as other directories known as subdirectories. Your instructor will show you where to find sample publications (called templates) necessary to complete the activities in this book.

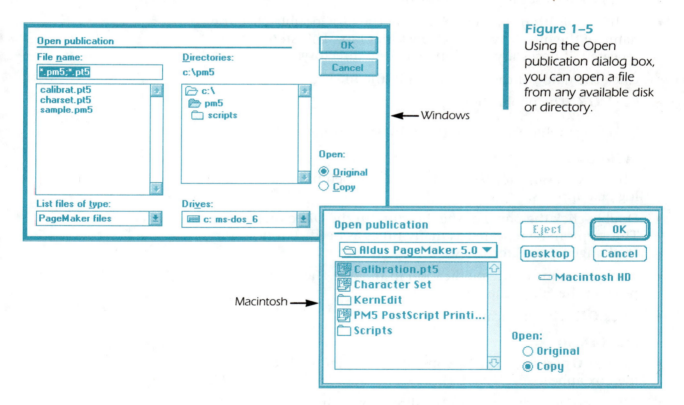

Figure 1–5
Using the Open publication dialog box, you can open a file from any available disk or directory.

To open a publication from a disk:

Windows

- Insert the disk.

- Choose **Open** from the **File** menu. The Open publication dialog box appears.

- In the Drives box, click on the arrow to drop down the menu.

- Double-click the drive letter of the disk that contains the file you want to open.

- If the publication is in a directory on the disk, double-click the name of the directory in the Directories box. This step can be repeated, if necessary, to go into a subdirectory.

- Click the name of the publication in the list under File name The filename appears in the File name box.

- Click **OK**. The publication opens.

Macintosh

- Insert the disk.

- Choose **Open** from the **File** menu. The Open publication dialog box appears.

- Click the **Desktop** button.

- Double-click on the name of the disk.

- If the publication is in a directory on the disk, double-click the name of the directory in the Directories box. This step can be repeated, if necessary, to change to a subdirectory.

- Click the name of the publication in the file list.

- Click **OK.** The publication opens.

To open a publication from the hard drive or network:

Windows

- Choose **Open** from the **File** menu. The Open publication dialog box appears.

- Double-click the name of the directory in the Directories box. This step can be repeated as many times as needed, if necessary, to change to subdirectories.

- Click the name of the publication in the list. The filename appears in the File name box.

- Click **OK.** The publication opens.

Macintosh

- Choose **Open** from the **File** menu. The Open publication dialog box appears.

- Click and hold the name of the directory at the top of the list of files. A list will drop down and will remain down as long as you hold down the mouse button.

- Drag the mouse down the list until the name of the directory you want becomes highlighted or darkened. You may need to select the name of the hard drive to find the list of files you need.

- Click the name of the publication in the file list.

- Click **OK.** The publication opens.

1. Find the location of the template files on the hard drive or network.
2. Change the current directory to *DTP*.
3. Open the publication **DEFINE**.
4. Leave the publication open for the next exercise.

EXERCISE 1-3

PRINTING A PUBLICATION

The Print command enables you to print your publication on paper.

To print a publication:

- Choose **Print** from the **File** menu. The Print document dialog box appears, as shown in Figure 1–6.

- Click **Print.**

N O T E

You can have as many publications open at the same time as the memory in your computer will allow.

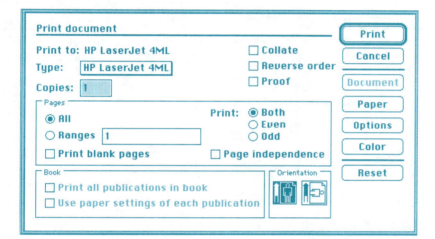

Figure 1–6
The Print document dialog box appears after you select the Print command.

1. Print the publication on your screen.
2. Leave the publication open for the next exercise.

EXERCISE 1-4

SAVING YOUR WORK

Saving is one of the most important features of any computer program. Files can be stored on a disk or on the hard drive of the computer.

You can save publications with the Save and Save As commands. The first time you save a publication, choose Save as from the File menu. PageMaker will automatically present the Save publication dialog box, shown in Figure 1–7. In this dialog box, type the new name of the file and the destination where you want PageMaker to save it. PageMaker will store the file in that location under the new name and then return to your publication.

The next time you want to save your publication, choose Save. Since the publication has already been saved for the first time, no dialog box will appear. PageMaker will save the current publication by overwriting the previous version of it.

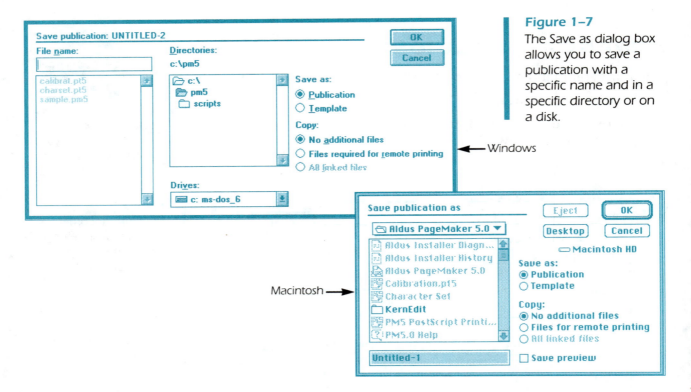

Figure 1–7
The Save as dialog box allows you to save a publication with a specific name and in a specific directory or on a disk.

To save a publication to a disk for the first time:

• Choose **Save as** from the **File** menu. The Save publication dialog box appears.

Windows

• Place your data disk in the drive.

• Click on the drive that contains your disk in the Drives box.

• Delete the existing filename from the File name box and key the new filename.

• Click **OK.** PageMaker saves the publication on your data disk.

Macintosh

• Place your data disk in the drive.

• Click on **Desktop.**

• Double-click on the name of your data disk.

• Delete the existing filename from the File name box and key the new filename.

• Click **OK.** PageMaker saves the publication on your data disk.

To save a publication to a hard drive or a network for the first time:

- Choose **Save as** from the **File** menu. The Save publication dialog box appears.

Windows

- Double-click on the directory name at the top of the directories box, which may be *C:*.
- Use the arrows to scroll down the list of subdirectories until you reach the one designated by your instructor as the site to save your files.
- Double-click on the name of the subdirectory.
- Delete the existing filename from the File name box and key the new filename.
- Click **OK**. PageMaker saves the publication to the new location.

Macintosh

- Click and hold the directory name at the top of the directory box. It is in a separate box. A list of directory names will be displayed as you hold down the mouse key.
- Continuing to hold the mouse key, scroll down the list of files in the directory until you reach the one designated by your instructor as the site to save your files.
- Release the mouse when the name becomes highlighted or darkened.
- Delete the existing filename from the File name box and key the new filename.
- Click **OK.** PageMaker saves the publication to the new location.

CLOSING A PUBLICATION

Closing a publication removes the publication from the screen and closes the file on the disk. If you have chosen any commands or have clicked on the publication window without saving, a dialog box like the one in Figure 1–8 will be displayed to ask if you want to save the changes to your publication before closing. If you want to save the changes, choose Yes. If you do not want to save the changes, choose No. If you decide not to close the publication, choose Cancel.

To close a publication:

- Choose **Close** from the **File** menu.

    -or-

Windows

- Double-click the close box.

    -or-

Macintosh

- Click the close box.

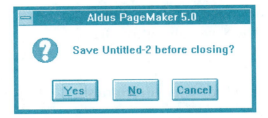

Figure 1–8
The Save changes box appears to warn you about modifications made in a publication.

ENDING A PAGEMAKER SESSION

End your PageMaker session by choosing Exit or Quit from the File menu. When you choose Exit or Quit, two operations occur. First, all PageMaker publications close. If you did not save one or more publications, you can save them at this point. Second, the Page-Maker program closes and you are returned to Microsoft Windows or the Macintosh desktop.

To exit PageMaker:

Windows

- Choose **Exit** from the **File** menu.

Macintosh

- Choose **Quit** from the **File** menu.

1. Save your publication as **EX1-5** to the location indicated by your instructor.

2. Close the publication.

3. End your PageMaker session.

EXERCISE 1–5

TRUE/FALSE

In the blank space before each sentence, place a **T** if the statement is true and an **F** if it is false.

_____ 1. When you start PageMaker, a new publication opens automatically.

_____ 2. Scroll bars are used when the file contains more information than the window can display.

_____ 3. Closing a publication erases your file.

_____ 4. To end your PageMaker session, choose Stop from the File menu.

_____ 5. You can choose Save as to give your existing file a different name or to save it to a new location.

COMPLETION

Fill in the blank.

6. How do you move to a specific page in a PageMaker publication?

_____

_____

7. On what part of the screen can you place text and then later move it onto a page?

_____

_____

8. From the toolbox, name four tools and their functions.

_____

_____

9. What are two ways to close a publication?

_____

_____

10. If a publication has already been saved for the first time, what will choosing the Save command do?

_____

_____

REVIEW EXERCISE 1–1

1. Start PageMaker and open a new publication.
2. Close the publication without saving it.
3. Access the Open publications dialog box.
4. Locate the template files. Change the current directory to *DTP*.
5. Open the publication **THOMAS.**
6. Print the publication.
7. Leave the publication open for the next review.

REVIEW EXERCISE 1–2

1. Close the publication **THOMAS.**
2. Open **FUN.**
3. Save the publication as **RE1-2** to the location indicated by your instructor.
4. Close the publication and end your PageMaker session.

LESSON 2

Text

After completing this lesson, you will be able to:

1. Change the view of a PageMaker publication.
2. Enter text.
3. Highlight text.
4. Delete, cut, copy, and paste text.
5. Undo your last command.
6. Import text.
7. Create a text block.
8. Move a text block.
9. Change the size of a text block.
10. Delete, cut, copy, and paste text blocks.

Estimated Time: 1 hour

CHANGING THE VIEW

PageMaker allows you to look at publications on the screen in many different views. New publications on your screen are shown in Fit in window view. You can also view publications at actual size and at 25%, 50%, 75%, 200%, and 400% of actual size, as shown in Figure 2–1. You can also show the entire pasteboard using the Show pasteboard command. Viewing the entire page is helpful when you want to work with the overall layout. When you are working on specific text, you will want a closer view.

To change the view of a publication:

- Choose **View** from the **Layout** menu.

- Click on the view you want.

Layout	
View	✓ Fit in window ^W
	Show pasteboard
Guides and rulers	
Column guides...	25% size ^0
	50% size ^5
Go to page... ^G	75% size ^7
Insert pages...	Actual size ^1
Remove pages...	200% size ^2
✓ Display master items	400% size ^4
Copy master guides	
Autoflow	

Figure 2–1
Change your view to fit your desktop-publishing need.

1. Create a new publication.

2. Change the view of the publication on your screen to actual size.

3. Change the view to **200%** size.

4. Change the view to **Fit in window.**

5. Close the publication without saving.

EXERCISE 2–1

ENTERING TEXT

When you want to key text in PageMaker, you will use the text tool from the Toolbox. The text tool is the A, as shown in Figure 2–2. When you select the text tool, it becomes a vertical line with curved top and bottom, called an I-beam. After you click it in place, a single pulsing line called a cursor replaces the I-beam.

Figure 2–2
Use the text tool to enter text into PageMaker.

To enter text:

- Click on the **text tool** in the toolbox. The pointer will change to an I-beam.

- Move the I-beam to the place where you want to begin keying and click.

- Key text.

1. Create a new publication.

2. Change the view of the publication on your screen to actual size.

3. Click on the screen with the text tool. An I-beam appears.

4. Key the following text.

   The main objectives of a layout are readability and visual appeal. Enliven a publication with graphics that relate to the text. A publication with a well-designed page layout can motivate the reader and keep their interest.

5. Save the publication as **EX2-2**.

6. Print the publication and leave it open for the next exercise.

HIGHLIGHTING TEXT

The text tool is also used to highlight or select text. Highlighting is used to select a body of text to be deleted, cut, or copied.

To highlight text:

- Using the text tool, move the pointer to the position where you want the selection to begin.

- Press the mouse button.

- Drag to highlight the text.

- Release the mouse button when the appropriate text has been highlighted.

DELETING, CUTTING, COPYING, AND PASTING TEXT

Once text is selected, you can manipulate it in a variety of ways. By pressing the Delete key, you can remove the text. By choosing Cut or Copy and then Paste from the Edit menu, as shown in Figure 2–3 on page 18, you can move the text.

To delete text:

- Using the text tool, highlight the text to be deleted.

- Press **Delete.**

Dragging is accomplished by holding down the mouse button and moving the pointer. On a two-button mouse, you will use the left button.

When you choose the Cut command, the text disappears from the screen and is placed on the Clipboard. The Clipboard is a temporary storage place in the computer's memory for text and graphics. You will not be able to see the material stored there.

To cut or copy text:

- Select the text with the text tool.

- Choose **Cut** or **Copy** from the **Edit** menu.

To move text from one location to another:

- Cut or copy the text.

- Move the cursor to the new location and press the mouse button.

- Choose **Paste** from the **Edit** menu.

UNDOING AN ACTION

If you accidentally delete, cut, or paste text, you can reverse the action by using the Undo command from the Edit menu. This command can only undo your last command or action.

To undo a command:

- Choose **Undo** from the **Edit** menu.

1. Highlight and delete the word *their* in the last line of your open publication.

2. Key **his or her** by placing the cursor after the word *keep,* being careful to leave a space between *keep* and *his.*

3. Highlight the second sentence, including the space after the period, and cut it.

4. Insert the cursor after the period at the end of the paragraph.

5. Press **Enter** twice to create a blank line between the paragraphs.

6. Paste the text.

7. Save the publication as **EX2-3.**

8. Print the publication and leave it open for the next exercise.

Figure 2–3
The Cut, Copy, and Paste commands allow you to move text from one place to another in a publication.

When you choose the Copy command, a copy of the selected text or graphic is placed on the Clipboard, leaving the original text unchanged.

A File menu command called Revert is similar to Undo. Revert allows you to return the publication to the last saved version.

EXERCISE 2–3

IMPORTING TEXT

The text tool is not designed to enter large amounts of text. It is best to create large publications in a word-processing program and then import them into your PageMaker publication using the Place command. PageMaker supports a wide variety of word-processing programs, which were selected during the installation process.

To place text:

- Choose **Place** from the **File** menu.

- When the Place document dialog box appears, choose the file you want to place.

- Select the options you want from the dialog box.

- Click **OK.**

- With a loaded cursor, like the one shown in Figure 2–4, click where you want the text to begin.

Figure 2–4
Click the loaded cursor in the spot where you want to place text.

EXERCISE 2–4

1. Place the cursor at the end of the last sentence.

2. Choose **Place** from the **File** menu.

3. From the template directory *TEXT*, select the publication **OBJ** by clicking once. Then click on the **Inserting text** option under **Place.**

4. Click **OK.**

5. The Text-only Import Filter will appear.

6. Click **OK.** Your open publication should now contain a page of text that begins, "The main objectives . . ."

7. Save the publication as **EX2-4.**

8. Print the publication and leave it open for the next exercise.

CREATING TEXT BLOCKS

When you key text into PageMaker, it becomes part of a story. A story is text that PageMaker considers a single unit. Publications can have one or many stories, and stories can be hundreds of pages long or contain only a single character.

Text blocks may contain an entire story or part of a story. The borders of a text block are horizontal lines with small squares on each end and handles in the middle. These borders with handles are called windowshades, as shown in Figure 2–5 (on page 20). You can see the windowshades only when a text block is selected.

NOTE

When you place text or graphics, PageMaker can establish a link to the original publication. This allows you to update your Page-Maker publication each time the original changes.

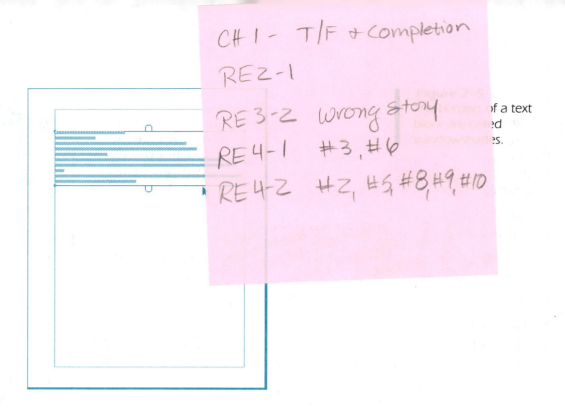

Figure 2–5 ... of a text block are called windowshades.

To select a text block, click on the text with the pointer tool. The windowshades appear. To deselect a text block, click outside the text block on a blank part of the page.

MOVING TEXT BLOCKS

While creating publications, you may move text blocks often to get them at just the right spot on the page. You can easily move text blocks with PageMaker.

To move a text block:

- Select the text block.

- Place the pointer anywhere on the text block.

- Press the mouse button and hold until the pointer becomes a four-sided arrow.

- Drag the text block to the new location.

CHANGING THE SIZE OF A TEXT BLOCK

Just as you may move text blocks around on the page, you may need to change the size of a text block to make all of the text fit in a certain spot or to achieve a certain design. PageMaker allows you to manipulate the size of text blocks easily using windowshade handles and corners. You can increase the width and/or height of a text block easily by dragging a windowshade corner. You can also make the text block longer. By looking at the windowshade handles, as shown in Figure 2–6, you can tell if text needs to be placed or the text block needs to be enlarged.

N O T E

Sometimes you may want to move a text block or graphic vertically or horizontally only. To do this, press and hold down the Shift key, then press the mouse button. The pointer will change to a two-sided arrow, and you can drag it to the new location.

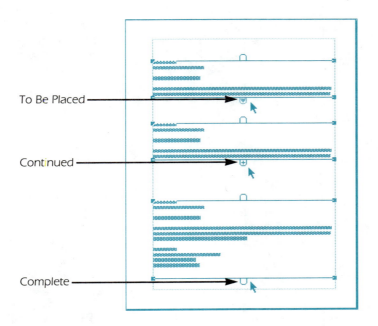

To Be Placed

Continued

Complete

Figure 2–6
Windowshade handles indicate if the story in the text block is complete, continued, or needs to be placed. A down arrow indicates text still needs to be placed. A plus sign shows that text has been continued elsewhere. An empty handle means that the text is complete.

To change the size of a text block:

- Select the text block.

- Place the pointer on a windowshade corner.

- Press the mouse button and hold until the pointer becomes a two-sided arrow.

- Drag in any direction to increase or decrease the width or height of the text block.

To make a text block longer:

- Position the pointer tool on the down arrow in the lower windowshade handle.

- Press the mouse button and drag downward.

1. Select the text block.

2. Change your view to **Fit in window.**

3. Change the size of the text block until it is approximately three inches wide. Use the rulers at the top of the page as a guide.

4. Observing the figure in the windowshade, make the text block long enough to include all the text.

5. Drag the text block to the lower-right corner, as shown in Figure 2–7 (on page 22).

6. Save the publication as **EX2-5.**

7. Print the publication and leave it open for the next exercise.

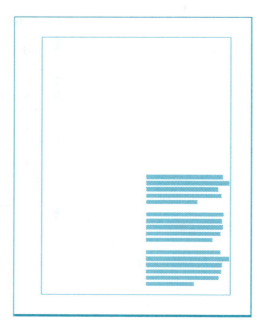

MANIPULATING TEXT BLOCKS

Just as you can manipulate text, you can delete, cut, copy, and paste an entire text block.

To delete an entire text block:

- Using the pointer tool, select the text block to be deleted.
- Press **Delete.**

To cut or copy and paste an entire text block:

- Use the pointer tool to select the text block to be cut or copied.
- Choose **Cut** or **Copy** from the **Edit** menu.
- Move the cursor to the new location and click.
- Choose **Paste** from the **Edit** menu.

N O T E

When you paste text or text blocks, you can click with either the text tool or the pointer tool in the spot where you want to paste the text. If you use the pointer tool, the text will be pasted exactly like the original text block on top of the original. You must then drag the text to the new position. If you use the text tool, the text will be pasted in a new text block that will not retain the size of the original text block.

EXERCISE 2–6

1. Copy the text block using the pointer tool. Paste it and move it to the top-left corner of the page.

2. Stretch the text block so that it is approximately twice the width of the text block at the bottom of the page.

3. Delete the text block at the bottom of the page. The text block disappears.

4. Undo the **Delete** command. The text block appears again.

5. Save the publication as **EX2-6.**

6. Print the publication and end your PageMaker session.

TRUE/FALSE

In the blank space before each sentence, place a **T** if the statement is true and an **F** if it is false.

_____ 1. A plus (+) symbol in the lower windowshade handle means that the rest of the story needs to be placed.

_____ 2. Highlighting text is also called selecting text.

_____ 3. The Edit and Paste commands are used to move text from one location to another.

_____ 4. The Copy command removes the original text from the screen.

_____ 5. The Undo command can only undo your last command or action.

COMPLETION

Fill in the blank.

6. What purpose does changing the view serve?

_____

_____

7. How do you delete an entire sentence from a text block?

_____

_____

8. What is the process for inserting a word in the middle of a paragraph?

_____

_____

9. Explain how to import text from a word-processing program.

_____

_____

10. How do you change the size of a text block?

_____

_____

Review Exercise 2–1

1. From the template directory *TEXT*, open the publication **PUPPIES**.

2. Select the text block.

3. Pull down the windowshade handle until all the text is showing.

4. Change the view to actual size.

5. Key **cute,** after *These*. (Be sure to leave one space between the comma and the word *healthy*.)

6. Key **915-** before *555* in the telephone number.

7. Place the cursor to the right of the *2* in the phone number and press **Enter** two times to create a blank line.

8. Highlight the two sentences that begin *These cute*.

9. Move the sentences to two lines below the phone number.

10. Delete one blank line before *Call Rich*. Now there should be two blank lines.

11. Copy the phone number and paste it in a new text block at the bottom of the page. Drag it in place so that it rests in the center of the page on the bottom margin line.

12. Key **Call** before the phone number at the bottom of the page.

13. Delete the line *Free to Good Homes!*

14. Undo the **Delete** command. Deselect the text.

15. Change the view to Fit in window.

16. Save the publication as **RE2-1.**

17. Print the publication and end your PageMaker session.

LESSON 3

The Story Editor

OBJECTIVES

After completing this lesson, you will be able to:

1. Use the story editor.
2. Check spelling.
3. Find and change text.
4. Display special characters.

Estimated Time: 1 hour

USING THE STORY EDITOR

The story editor is PageMaker's word-processing center. In the story editor, you can key in or change text, check spelling, search and replace, and perform other editing functions as you would in a word-processing program. Until now, you have been working in layout view, which provides only limited editing functions.

In the story editor, text is shown without formatting such as tabs or type styles. See Figure 3–1. The text is shown in the font and size specified in the Preferences dialog box. Style names and special characters may also be shown in the story editor.

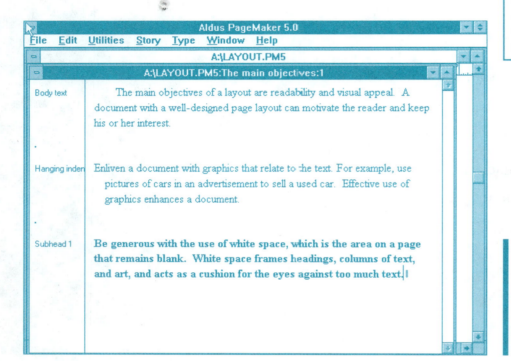

Figure 3–1
The story editor shows text set in a standard size and font. If you change the size, it will not be apparent until you leave the story editor.

To edit the story of an existing text block:

- Click an insertion point with the text tool I-beam anywhere in a text block.

  -or-

  Select the text block with the pointer tool.

- Choose **Edit story** from the **Edit** menu.

To close the story editor and return to layout view:

- Choose **Close story** from the **Story** menu.

  -or-

  Close the window.

  -or-

  Choose **Edit layout** from the **Edit** menu.

To create a new story:

- Make sure nothing is selected.
- Choose **Edit story** from the **Edit** menu.
- Key your information.

To place a new story created in story editor:

- Close the story.
- Click on **Place** when the Place dialog box appears, as shown in Figure 3–2. A loaded cursor will appear when you return to the PageMaker screen.
- Click the cursor where you wish to locate the text.
- Deselect the text.

Figure 3–2
The Place dialog box prompts you to place the new story onto your PageMaker publication.

▶ **EXERCISE 3-1**

1. From the template directory *STORY*, open **HISTORY.**
2. Select the text block with the pointer tool.
3. Choose **Edit story** from the **Edit** menu.
4. Close the story.
5. Create a new story. Key in **History of Computers.**
6. Place the story above the existing text block.
7. Save the publication as **EX3-1.**
8. Print the publication and leave it open for the next exercise.

USING STORY EDITOR UTILITIES

One of the story editor's most important functions allows you to check spelling and find and change words. These editing features are in the Utilities menu of the story editor.

Spell Checker

PageMaker checks the spellings of words in your publication against its dictionary. When it finds a word not in its dictionary, a misspelled word, a possible capitalization error, or a double word error, it prompts you to ignore, replace, or add the word to the dictionary.

The Spelling dialog box, as shown in Figure 3–3, gives you the option to check the spelling in selected text, one story in a publication, all stories in a publication, or all stories in all open publications. PageMaker checks spelling only. It will not find grammatical errors.

Figure 3–3
The Spelling dialog box allows you to check the spellings of words, ignore words, change misspelled words, or add words to the dictionary.

To check spelling:

- In story editor, choose **Spelling** from the **Utilities** menu. The Spelling dialog box appears.
- Check the options that tell PageMaker what parts of your publication(s) you want to check for spelling errors.
- Choose **Start.**
- When PageMaker stops on a word, click **Ignore** to continue without making a change or choose a word from the **Change to** list and click **Replace.** You can also key in the correct spelling of a word in the **Change to** box.
- Close the window.

N O T E

Checking the spelling of a publication does not replace proofreading. If you key "form" instead of "from," the spelling checker will not detect the error.

1. Select the largest text block.
2. Open the story editor.
3. Use the **Spelling Checker** to check the spelling of the publication.
4. Return to the layout view.
5. Save the publication as **EX3-2.**
6. Print the publication and leave it open for the next exercise.

▶ **EXERCISE 3–2**

Find

The Find command lets you quickly search a publication for every occurrence of a specific character, word, or phrase. Find moves the cursor from its current position to the next occurrence of the word or phrase for which you are searching. As with the spell-checking feature, you can choose to search only the selected text, one story in a publication, all stories in a publication, or all stories in all open publications.

To find a character, word, or phrase:

- In story editor, make sure no text is highlighted. Choose **Find** from the **Utilities** menu. The Find dialog box appears as shown in Figure 3–4.

- In the *Find what:* box key the word or phrase you want to find.

- Click **Find.** PageMaker will highlight the next occurrence.

- Click **Find next** to continue the search; click outside the box or use the close box to stop Find.

- Close the window.

Figure 3–4
The Find dialog box is used to find a specific character, word, or phrase in a publication.

The Find command can find whole or partial words. For example, PageMaker can find the word *all* or any word with *all* in it, such as *fall, horizontally,* or *alloy.* Find can look for words that match a specific capitalization. For example, if you wanted to search for the word *page* in lowercase letters, you would click Match case in the Find dialog box. PageMaker would find *page,* but not *Page* or *PAGE.*

The Attributes option helps you find words that have specific characteristics. Using the Find attributes dialog box, shown in Figure 3–5, you can specify the paragraph style, font, size, and/or type style of the word you want to find.

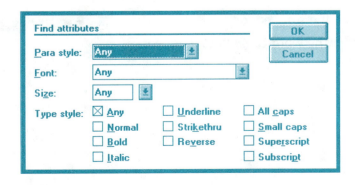

Figure 3–5
The Find attributes dialog box helps you locate words with specific formatting characteristics.

Change

The Change command is an extended version of the Find command. Change has all the features of Find. In addition, however, the Change dialog box, shown in Figure 3–6, allows you to replace a word or phrase with another word or phrase that you specify. The changes can be done individually, or all occurrences can be changed at once.

As with the Find command, the Change command also has an Attributes option to let you search for a word with specific characteristics then change the word to another word with specific characteristics.

Figure 3–6
The Change dialog box contains options you can use to replace a word found with a new word.

To find and change characters, words, or phrases:

- In story editor, make sure no text is highlighted. Choose **Change** from the **Utilities** menu. The Change dialog box appears.
- Key the word or phrase you want to change in the *Find what:* box.
- In the *Change to:* box, key the replacement for the word or phrase.
- Choose **Find** to go to the first occurrence. You will be asked at each occurrence if you want to change it. To continue changing the words one by one, choose **Change & find.**

  -or-

  Choose **Change all** to replace all occurrences with no prompts.
- Close the window.

1. Select the largest text block and open the story editor.

2. Search *all* stories in the publication for the word *computers*. It appears four times.

EXERCISE 3-3

3. Search *all* stories in the publication for the word *Computers* using the Match Case option. It appears once.

4. Use the **Change** command to find and replace all occurrences of the word *Now* with the word *Today*. One occurrence will be replaced.

5. Return to layout view.

6. Save the publication as **EX3-3.**

7. Print the publication and leave it open for the next exercise.

Special Characters

The Display ¶ command is used to view hidden formatting characters in the story editor. (This command is not available in layout view.) These are hidden special characters such as spaces, paragraph markers, or new-line marks, as shown in Figure 3–7. Being able to see these hidden characters can help you in editing your text.

To display hidden characters:

- In story editor, choose **Display ¶** from the **Story** menu. The hidden special characters appear.

To hide the characters:

- In story editor, Choose **Display ¶** from the **Story** menu again. The special characters disappear.

N O T E

Frequently you will turn on a command by selecting it and turn it off by selecting it again. This "toggle" function is used with commands such as Display ¶.

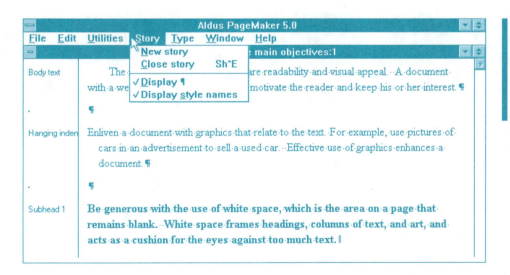

Figure 3–7

Choosing the Display ¶ command from the story editor's Story menu makes hidden formatting characters appear.

1. Select the largest text block and open the story editor.

2 Show the hidden formatting characters.

3. Hide the formatting characters.

4. Return to layout view.

5. End your PageMaker session.

TRUE/FALSE

In the blank space before each sentence, place a **T** if the statement is true and an **F** if it is false.

_____ 1. You can perform more editing functions in the story editor than you can in layout view.

_____ 2. When you place a new story created in the story editor, you use a loaded cursor.

_____ 3. PageMaker's spelling checker finds grammatical errors.

_____ 4. PageMaker can only check the spelling of a single text block.

_____ 5. The Find command is an extended version of the Change command.

COMPLETION

Fill in the blank.

6. How do you open a new story in story editor?

_____

_____

7. What does the Match case option in the Find dialog box do?

_____

_____

8. Which option in the Change dialog box allows you to replace all occurrences without prompts?

_____

_____

9. Which two commands give you an Attributes option?

_____

_____

10. What are two examples of hidden formatting characters?

_____

_____

REVIEW EXERCISE 3–1

1. Create a new publication using the default settings.

2. In the upper-left corner of your page, place **EXERCISE** from the *STORY* directory.

3. Go to the story editor and check the spelling.

4. Find the words *worn out* and change them to *sluggish*.

5. Show the hidden characters.

6. Insert a blank line (paragraph) after the title, *Why Exercise?*

7. Return to layout view.

8. Move the text block down until it is approximately centered on the page.

9. Save the publication as **RE3-1**.

10. Print the publication and close it.

REVIEW EXERCISE 3–2

1. Create a new publication using the default settings.

2. At the upper-left corner of your page within the margins, place **GARAGE** from the *STORY* directory.

3. Open the story editor.

4. Change *Beverly* to *Tom*.

5. Delete the two paragraph markers at the bottom of the page.

6. Hide hidden characters.

7. Check the spelling.

8. Return to layout view.

9. Highlight all text.

10. Copy the entire text block.

11. Paste the text block below the first one, at the bottom of the page.

12. Save the publication as **RE3-2**.

13. Print the publication and end your PageMaker session.

LESSON 4

Advanced Text

OBJECTIVES

After completing this lesson, you will be able to:

1. Choose fonts.
2. Change the size of type.
3. Change the type style of text.
4. Choose an appropriate alignment for text.
5. Use leading.
6. Use tracking.
7. Kern characters automatically and manually.
8. Change the width of characters.
9. Change text characteristics using the Type Specs command.

Estimated Time: 1 hour

Until now, you have been learning how to import text and manipulate it. Now you are ready to learn how to change the look of your text.

CHOOSING FONTS

The term *font* refers to the shapes of the characters belonging to a particular family of type. A font is also called a typeface. A typeface with small lines added to the ends of the characters is called a *serif* typeface and is best used for main body text. A typeface without serifs is called a *sans serif* typeface and is good to use for headlines (see Figure 4–1).

Your printer determines what fonts are available to you. If your printer has cartridges or downloadable fonts available, you may have a wide variety of fonts from which to choose. Or, you may find that you have only one or two fonts.

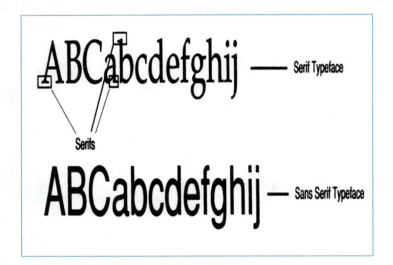

Serifs

To change a font:

- Highlight the text to be changed with the text tool.
- Choose **Font** from the **Type** menu.
- Click on the name of the font.

1. Open **TYPTERM** from the *TEXT* directory.
2. Highlight the title of the publication.
3. Change the font to **Arial** or **Helvetica.** If neither of these fonts is available, choose another sans serif font designated by your instructor.
4. Highlight the body of the publication. (All except the title.)

Figure 4–1
A serif typeface has small lines added to the ends of characters. Sans serif typefaces do not have the lines.

EXERCISE 4–1

5. Change the font to **Times New Roman.** If this font is not available, choose another serif font.

6. Save the publication as **EX4-1.**

7. Print the publication and leave it open for the next exercise.

CHANGING TYPE SIZE

The size of type is determined by measuring its height in units called points. There are 72 points per inch. A common size for type is 12 point. Different sizes of the same typeface can be selected.

To change the size of text:

• Highlight the text you want to change with the text tool.

• Choose **Size** from the **Type** menu.

• Click on the size you want.

1. Highlight the title of the publication.

2. Change the size to **14 point.**

3. Highlight the body of the publication (all of it except the title).

4. Change the size to **12 point.**

5. Save the publication as **EX4-2.**

6. Print the publication and leave it open for the next exercise.

CHANGING TYPE STYLE

Type style refers to certain changes in the appearance of a font. Type styles available in PageMaker are boldface, italic, underline, strikethru, outline, shadow, and reverse, as shown in Figure 4–2 (on page 38). These styles can be applied to change the appearance of any font.

When you begin keying a publication in the word processor, you are using a normal style. This is the style you will most likely use for the body of your publication. However, you might want to use other styles for particular features in your publication. For example, you could emphasize a specific word by applying a boldface style to it. More than one style can be applied to the same text. For example, you can boldface and italicize text.

Because italic, underlined, and strikethru text are harder to read than normal text, avoid over using them in a publication. Overusing type styles for emphasis can actually take away the emphasis you were trying to achieve.

To change the style of text:

• Highlight the text you want to change with the text tool.

• Choose **Type style** from the **Type** menu.

• Click on the type style you want.

N O T E

If text is highlighted when you choose a font, the highlighted text will take on the new font. If no text is highlighted, the new font will be in effect as you key new text.

▶ **EXERCISE 4–2**

N O T E

Like changing the font, changing the style affects the highlighted text or will affect text that is keyed after the style is chosen.

This is an example of plain text.

This is an example of bold text.

This is an example of italic text.

This is an example of underlined text.

~~This is an example of strikethru text.~~

This is an example of outline text.

This is an example of shadow text.

Figure 4–2
Type styles are used to emphasize text.

You might find keyboard shortcuts to be the best way to change the style of text. Table 4–1 shows the shortcuts that can be used as alternatives to choosing the type style from the menu.

Table 4–1

Style	Windows Shortcut	Macintosh Shortcut
Bold	Shift + Ctrl + B	Shift + Command + B
Italic	Shift + Ctrl + I	Shift + Command + I
Underline	Shift + Ctrl + U	Shift + Command + U
Strikethru	Shift + Ctrl + /	Shift + Command + /
Outline	None	Shift + Command + D
Shadow	None	Shift + Command + W
Normal	Shift + Ctrl + Space bar	Shift + Command + Space bar
Reverse	Shift + Ctrl + V	Shift + Command + Space bar

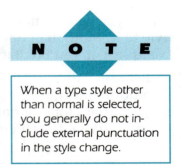

N O T E

When a type style other than normal is selected, you generally do not include external punctuation in the style change.

1. Boldface the title of the publication.

2. Boldface the subheading *Characters* and all other subheadings in the publication.

3. Italicize the word *character* in the first sentence of the first paragraph.

4. Italicize *baseline* in the first sentence of the second paragraph.

5. Italicize *descender* in the first sentence of the third paragraph. Also italicize the characters *g* and *y* in the next sentence.

6. Italicize *x-height* in the second sentence of the fourth paragraph.

7. Italicize *ascender* in the first sentence of the fifth paragraph and the characters *f* and *k* in the next sentence.

8. Italicize *cap height* in the first sentence of the sixth paragraph.

9. Italicize *serifs* in the second sentence of the seventh paragraph. Also italicize *sans serif* in the fourth sentence of the seventh paragraph.

10. Save the publication as **EX4-3.**

11. Print the publication and leave it open for the next exercise.

► **EXERCISE 4–3**

SETTING ALIGNMENT

Choosing alignment allows you to center text, justify text, or place text flush against the right or left margin. It does not allow you to move text vertically on the page. The default alignment is flush left. To change the alignment, use the Alignment command from the Type menu, as shown in Figure 4–3.

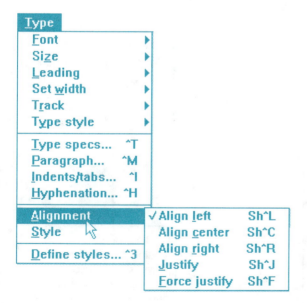

Figure 4–3
The alignment menu lets you modify the placement of text on a line. Examples of alignment are shown.

To use the Alignment command:

- Highlight the text you want to align with the text tool.
- Choose **Alignment** from the **Type** menu.
- Click the option you want.

1. Highlight the title of the publication.
2. Change the alignment to **Align center.**
3. Highlight the body of the publication.
4. Change the alignment to **Justify.**
5. Save the publication as **EX4-4.**
6. Print the publication and leave it open for the next exercise.

CHANGING LEADING

Spacing is an important part of page layout. Adding or subtracting space in text can visually enhance your publication. The amount of vertical space between lines of type is called leading. When you want to change leading, you use the Leading command from the Type menu, as shown in Figure 4–4. The default leading is Auto, which sets the leading at a number 20 percent greater than the size of the font you are using.

The default setting is the equivalent of single spacing text. To double-space your text, set the leading at twice the default number. You can change the leading between single lines or all of the lines in a paragraph.

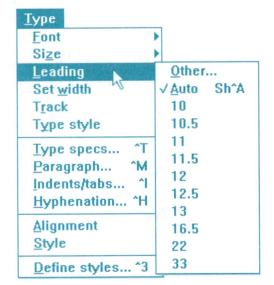

Figure 4–4
The Leading command allows you to change the spacing between lines of text, which can make the text easier to read.

Leading, pronounced ledding, comes from the printer's term indicating the placement of lead strips between lines of text.

To use the Leading command:

- Highlight the text you want to change with the text tool.

- Choose **Leading** from the **Type** menu.

- Click on the leading you want.

  -or-

  Click **Other,** key in the number you want, and click on **OK.**

▶ **EXERCISE 4–5**

1. Highlight the body of the publication, including the title.

2. Change the leading to **21.**

3. Save the publication as **EX4-5.**

4. Print the publication and close it.

SELECTING TRACKING

The Track command lets you change the amount of space between characters. PageMaker gives you choices that range from Very loose to Very tight, as shown in Figure 4–5. The default tracking is No track, which uses the built-in spacing of the font you are using.

You can use tracking to create special effects or to adjust the spacing for very large or very small type. Tracking can also be useful when you need to fit type into a specified space. You can use tracking to change the space between individual characters or all characters in a paragraph.

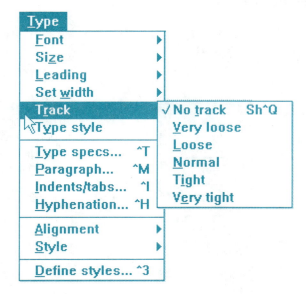

Figure 4–5
Tracking lets you adjust the amount of space between characters.

To apply tracking:

- Highlight the text you want to track with the text tool.
- Choose **Track** from the **Type** menu.
- Click on the tracking option you want.

EXERCISE 4–6

1. Open **TRACK** from the *TEXT* directory.
2. Set the tracking on *New York* to **Normal.** Now the two words fit on one line.
3. Save the publication as **EX4-6.**
4. Print the publication and leave it open for the next exercise.

ADJUSTING KERNING

Kerning adjusts the spacing between specialized characters. Letters that are frequently kerned include LA, Po, To, Tr, Ta, Tu, Te, Ty, Wa, WA, We, we, Wo, Ya, Yo, and yo, because they can fit together more closely than can other letters. These letter groups are visually more attractive when the extra space is removed. Generally you need to kern only text that is very noticeable—usually large type such as that in headlines. PageMaker lets you kern manually or automatically.

Automatic Kerning

Automatic kerning can be applied to one paragraph or to all paragraphs in a publication. You cannot apply it to only a few characters in a paragraph.

To kern character pairs automatically:

- Highlight the paragraph(s) with the text tool.
- Choose **Paragraph** from the **Type** menu.
- Choose **Spacing** from the Paragraph specifications dialog box (see Figure 4–6).

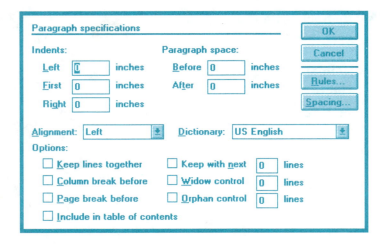

Figure 4–6
The Paragraph specifications dialog box gives you access to spacing.

- Click in the box beside **Auto above** in the Spacing attributes dialog box, as shown in Figure 4–7.

- Key a size in the **points** box above which you want PageMaker to kern pairs.

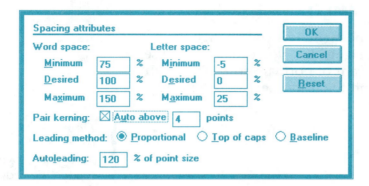

Figure 4–7
The Spacing attributes dialog box allows you to adjust kerning.

Manual Kerning

Manual kerning allows you to kern only specific characters in a paragraph.

To increase spacing by 1/25 em between character pairs manually:

- Insert the text tool cursor between the two characters.

Windows

- Press **Ctrl + "+"** (plus on the numeric keypad) or **Ctrl + Shift + Backspace.**

-or-

Macintosh

- Press **Command + Shift + Delete** or **Command + Right arrow.**

To decrease spacing by 1/25 em between character pairs manually:

- Position the cursor between the two characters and click.

Windows

- Press **Ctrl + "-"** (minus on the numeric keypad) or **Backspace** or **Ctrl.**

-or-

Macintosh

- Press **Command + Delete** or **Command + Left arrow.**

N O T E

An em is a printer's term for a horizontal space approximately one-sixth of an inch. An en is half the space of an em.

1. Highlight *Texas.* Notice the extra space between the *T* and *e.*

2. Turn on automatic kerning. Key **24** as the point size above which to kern. The space between the *T* and *e* is decreased.

3. Notice the extra space between the *Y* and the *o* in *New York.*

EXERCISE 4–7

4. Use manual kerning to reduce the space by 2/25 em (two spaces).

5. Save the publication as **EX4-7.**

6. Print the publication and leave it open for the next exercise.

SETTING CHARACTER WIDTH

The Set width command in the Type menu lets you change the widths of characters. As shown in Figure 4–8, you can choose to set widths from 70 percent to 130 percent of normal width. You might want to use the Set width command to create special text effects.

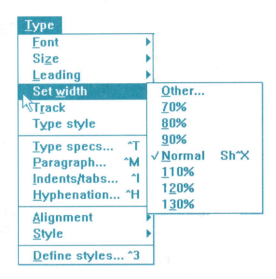

Figure 4–8
The Set Width command lets you change the widths of characters to create special text effects.

To set the widths of characters:

*   Highlight the characters or text with the text tool.

*   Choose **Set Width** from the **Type** menu.

*   Click on the character width you want.

NOTE

You can specify a character width other than those listed by choosing Other from the list of widths and keying the new percentage.

1. Set the width on the word *Texas* to **120%.**

2. Set the width on the words *New York* to **80%.**

3. Save the publication as **EX4-8.**

4. Print the publication and leave it open for the next exercise.

EXERCISE 4–8

CHANGING TYPE SPECS

When you want to change several text attributes at the same time, you can use the Type Specs command from the Type menu. The Type specifications dialog box, shown in Figure 4–9, allows you to change many characteristics of text at the same time.

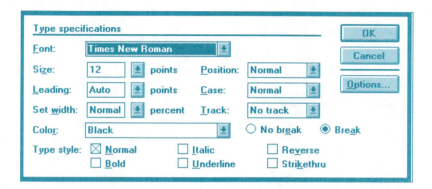

Figure 4–9
The Type specifications dialog box allows you to change the font, size, type style, and other characteristics of text at the same time.

To use the Type specs command:

• Highlight the text you want to change with the text tool.

• Choose **Type specs** from the **Type** menu.

• Click and change the options you want.

N O T E

In the Type specifications dialog box, you can change text to a size not listed by keying the new point size in the size box. You can even key in a point size in increments of one-tenth of a point, such as 12.5.

EXERCISE 4–9

1. Highlight the body of the publication.

2. Using **Type specs,** change the type style to **Bold.**

3. Change the size to 135.

4. Save the publication as **EX4-9.**

5. Print the publication and end your PageMaker session.

TRUE/FALSE

In the blank space before each sentence, place a **T** if the statement is true and an **F** if it is false.

_____ 1. A font is also called a typeface.

_____ 2. The size of type is determined by measuring its height in units called points.

_____ 3. You can emphasize a word by applying a boldface style to it.

_____ 4. Choosing justified text centers text between the right and left margins.

_____ 5. The Set width command changes the amount of space between characters.

COMPLETION

Fill in the blank.

6. What determines the fonts that are available on your computer?

    _____

    _____

7. If no text is highlighted when a font is chosen, what is affected by the new font choice?

    _____

    _____

8. How are tracking and kerning different?

    _____

    _____

9. When would you need to use more leading?

    _____

    _____

10. What does the Type specifications dialog box allow you to do?

    _____

    _____

REVIEW EXERCISE 4–1

1. Open **BDAY** from the *TEXT* directory.

2. Change the alignment to Align center.

3. Change the size of the text block to match the page margins.

4. Boldface *Hannah Richards*.

5. Italicize the last line, which begins *Please limit.*

6. Using Type specs, change the font of the entire text block to Times New Roman or a similar serif font, the size to 30 points, and set the width to 90%.

7. Adjust the placement of the text block if needed.

8. Save the publication as **RE4-1.**

9. Print the publication and close it.

REVIEW EXERCISE 4–2

1. Open **QUESTION** from the *TEXT* directory.

2. Using Type specs, change the size of the text in the block that begins *Do YOU* to 72 points, change the tracking to Very loose, and boldface the text.

3. Change the text at the bottom of the page to 24 points.

4. Change the alignment to justify.

5. Change the leading to 36 points.

6. Move the text block so that the bottom line rests on the bottom margin.

7. Of the three large question marks on the right side of the page, change the size of the top question mark to 100 points.

8. Change the size of the middle question mark to 200 points and set its width to 130%.

9. Change the size of the bottom question mark to 150 points and change its width to 110%.

10. Use kerning to decrease the space 2/25 em between the *Y* and *O* in *YOU.*

11. Save the publication as **RE4-2.**

12. Print the publication and end your PageMaker session.

LESSON 5

Graphics

OBJECTIVES

After completing this lesson, you will be able to:

1. Cut, paste, and copy objects.
2. Import objects.
3. Draw squares, rectangles, circles, ovals, and lines.
4. Apply fill and line to selected objects.
5. Layer objects.

Estimated Time: 1 hour

CUTTING, PASTING, AND COPYING OBJECTS

You can cut, paste, and copy drawings and other graphics using the same basic methods you did with text. If you need to move an object on a page, you simply select the object and drag it to the new location. If you need to move an object to another page or document, you can use the Cut and Paste commands.

To move or copy an independent graphic from one page or document to another:

- Using the pointer tool, select the object you want to move.
- Choose **Cut** or **Copy** from the **Edit** menu.
- Move to the new page or document.
- Choose **Paste** from the **Edit** menu. The object reappears.
- Drag the object into place.

Inline Graphics

An inline graphic differs from an independent graphic in that it is an object embedded in the text. If you want to move an inline graphic from one location to another, you can use the Cut and Paste commands. Just be sure to place the cursor in the text where you want the graphic to appear.

1. Open **ICECREAM** from the *GRAPHICS* directory.
2. Select the ice cream cone on the pasteboard and cut it.
3. Paste it into the text line after the word *galore*. Add a space. It is now an inline graphic rather than an independent one.
4. Move the ice cream sundae in the empty area to the left of the text that begins *Come join us*.
5. Save the publication as **EX5-1**.
6. Print the publication and leave it open for the next exercise.

IMPORTING OBJECTS

Just as you can import text, you can import objects that have been created using a variety of graphics programs. Once you have imported these objects, they can be somewhat modified using Page-Maker tools.

To import an object:

- Choose **Place** from the **File** menu.
- Choose the file you want to place.
- Select the options you want from the dialog box.

An independent graphic is a figure that can be moved around the page independent of a text block. An inline graphic is one that becomes part of the text block.

The Multiple paste command from the Edit menu is useful when you want more than one copy of an object on the same page.

EXERCISE 5–1

Once an inline graphic is embedded into text, it becomes a part of a text block and will move with the text.

PageMaker imports a variety of graphic formats: BMP, PCX, CGM, WMF, PNT, PICT, TIFF, and EPS.

- Click **OK.**
- With a loaded cursor like the one shown in Figure 5–1, click where you want the object to be placed.

Figure 5–1
Click the loaded cursor in the spot where you want to place your graphic.

1. Place your cursor after the word *fruit.*
2. Choose **Place** from the **File** menu.
3. Select **STRBERRY** from the directory *GRAPHICS* by clicking twice. Make sure the **As independent graphic** option under **Place** is checked. A loaded cursor will appear.
4. Click anywhere on the pasteboard to place the graphic.
5. Copy the strawberry.
6. Place the cursor after the word *fruit.* Paste the graphic.
7. Save the publication as **EX5-2.**
8. Print the publication and close it.

N O T E

Since PageMaker can establish a graphic or text link to the original publication, you can modify a graphic after you import it.

DRAWING SIMPLE GRAPHICS

You can create your own simple graphics in PageMaker. The Toolbox shown in Figure 5–2 contains the rectangle tool, ellipse tool, and line tools to help you.

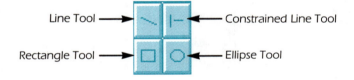

Line Tool →   ← Constrained Line Tool

Rectangle Tool →   ← Ellipse Tool

Figure 5–2
The line tool, constrained-line tool, ellipse tool, and rectangle tool are used for creating graphics.

Rectangles and Squares

You can draw any size rectangle with the rectangle tool, or you can draw a perfect square. To draw an object of an exact size or at an exact location, choose the appropriate tool and position it at what will be the uppermost left point of the object. Click and drag diagonally to the lower-right point of the object. When you drag the tool, you will notice the dotted lines on the ruler move with the tool to indicate your location and size on the page.

To draw a rectangle:
- Select the **rectangle tool** in the Toolbox. The pointer turns into a crossbar.
- Click and drag.

To draw a square:
- Select the **rectangle tool** in the Toolbox. The pointer turns into a crossbar.

- Press the **Shift** key and hold.
- Click and drag to draw a square.

EXERCISE 5–3

1. Create a new document using the default settings.

2. Draw a rectangle. Begin at the 3-inch mark on the horizontal ruler guide and at the 1-1/2-inch mark on the vertical ruler guide. Drag the rectangle to the 6-inch mark on the horizontal ruler guide and the 3-inch mark on the vertical ruler.

3. Place a 1-inch square in the middle of the rectangle. Your screen should look like Figure 5–3.

4. Save the publication as **EX5-3.**

5. Print the publication and leave it open for the next exercise.

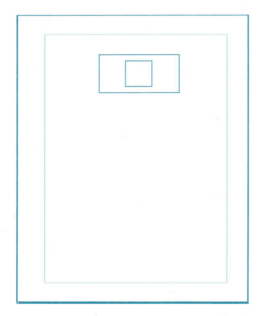

Figure 5–3
You can draw rectangles and squares with the rectangle tool.

Circles and Ovals

With the ellipse tool, you can draw various sizes and shapes of ovals. You can also draw perfect circles.

To draw an oval:

- Select the **ellipse tool** from the Toolbox. The pointer turns into a crossbar.
- Click and drag.

To draw a circle:

- Select the **ellipse** tool in the Toolbox. The tool turns into a crossbar.
- Press the **Shift** key and hold.
- Click and drag.

1. Draw a 3/4-inch circle and place it inside the square you drew in the last activity.

2. Draw an oval approximately 1/2-inch wide by 1/4-inch tall.

3. Place it in the upper-right corner of the rectangle. Your screen should look like Figure 5–4.

4. Save the publication as **EX5-4.**

5. Print the publication and leave it open for the next exercise.

▶ **EXERCISE 5–4**

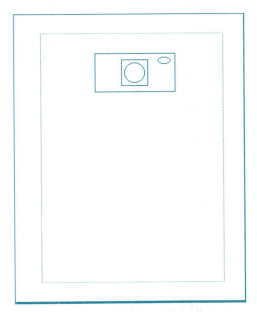

Figure 5–4
You can draw circles and ovals with the ellipse tool.

Lines

You can draw straight and angled lines with PageMaker's line and constrained-line tools. The line tool draws straight lines at any angle. The constrained-line tool draws straight lines at 45-degree angles.

To draw a straight line at any angle:

- Select the **line tool** from the Toolbox.

- Click and drag.

To draw a straight line at a 45-degree angle:

- Select the **constrained-line tool** from the Toolbox.

- Click and drag.

1. Use the constrained-line tool to draw a vertical straight line from the bottom middle of the rectangle to the 8-1/2-inch vertical guide. By now you may see that the object you are creating is a camera.

2. Use the line tool to draw an angled line from the bottom middle of the camera to the 9-inch ruler guide at the right margin of the page.

▶ **EXERCISE 5–5**

3. Draw another angled line from the bottom middle of the camera to the 9-inch ruler guide at the left margin of the page. Your screen should look like Figure 5–5.

4. Save the publication as **EX5-5.**

5. Print the publication and leave it open for the next exercise.

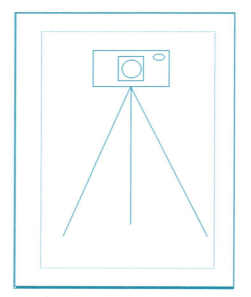

Figure 5–5
You can draw straight lines using the line tools.

CHANGING THE LINE AND FILL

You can change the appearance of ovals, circles, rectangles, and lines by changing line types and weights and by filling the objects with patterns. You have a choice of many different types and sizes of lines in the Line pull-down menu, as shown in Figure 5–6. Reverse makes a line white.

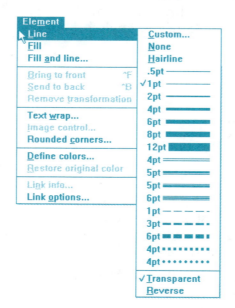

Figure 5–6
The Line pull-down menu lists many different line types and weights.

To change a line:

- Select the line.
- Choose **Line** from the **Element** menu.
- Choose the line style or weight that you want.

You can fill any object using the patterns in the Fill pull-down menu shown in Figure 5–7. A graphic without a fill pattern is transparent—it lets other objects show through it. A paper fill pattern hides other objects even though it appears clear.

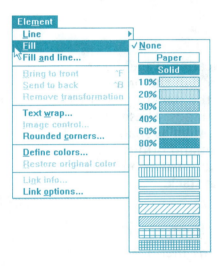

To change the fill:

- Select the object.
- Choose **Fill** from the **Element** menu.
- Choose the fill pattern that you want.

You can change both the fill and line at the same time using the Fill and line dialog box, shown in Figure 5–8.

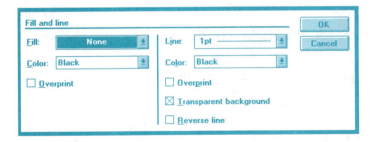

To change the fill and line at the same time:

- Select the object.
- Choose **Fill and line** from the **Element** menu. The Fill and line dialog box appears.
- Choose the line and fill you want.
- Choose **OK.**

1. Select the middle line of the tripod.

2. Change the line weight to 4 points.

3. Change the line weights of the other two lines of the tripod to 4 points.

4. Fill the oval with a 20-percent shade.

5. Fill the circle with the small diagonal lines pattern.

6. Save the publication as **EX5-6.**

7. Print the publication and leave it open for the next exercise.

EXERCISE 5–6

LAYERING GRAPHICS

As items are created or imported into a publication, PageMaker gives them a stacking order from bottom to top in the order they were created or imported. You can rearrange the stacking order using the Bring to front and Send to back commands. These commands allow you to create interesting effects, such as shadows and backgrounds for text. The Bring to front command brings the selected object to the top of the stack. The Send to back command sends the selected object to the bottom of the stack.

To use the Bring to front command:

• Select the object you want to bring to the front.

• Choose **Bring to front** from the **Element** menu. The object moves to the top of the stacking order.

To use the Send to back command:

• Select the object you want to send to back.

• Choose **Send to back** from the **Element** menu. The object moves to the bottom of the stacking order.

1. Fill the square with the paper fill.

2. Fill the large rectangle with solid black.

3. Select the square and send it to the back. The black rectangle hides the square.

4. With the square still selected, bring the square to the front. The square hides the circle.

5. Send the square to the back.

6. Select the rectangle. Send it to the back.

7. Save the publication as **EX5-7.**

8. Print the publication and end your PageMaker session.

EXERCISE 5–7

TRUE/FALSE

In the blank space before each sentence, place a **T** if the statement is true and an **F** if it is false.

_____ 1. The Toolbox contains the tools for drawing rectangles, ellipses, and lines.

_____ 2. An inline graphic can be moved independently of text.

_____ 3. The ellipse tool lets you draw circles.

_____ 4. The constrained-line tool draws straight lines at any angle.

_____ 5. PageMaker gives objects a stacking order from bottom to top in the order they were created or imported.

COMPLETION

Fill in the blank.

6. What purpose does the Line pull-down menu serve?

_____

_____

7. How do you place an inline graphic?

_____

_____

8. How do you draw a perfect square?

_____

_____

9. What does a paper fill do?

_____

_____

10. Which two commands change the stacking order of objects?

_____

_____

Review Exercise 5–1

1. Open **BULLSEYE** from the directory *GRAPHICS*.

2. Fill the smallest circle with solid black.

3. Fill the next smallest circle with paper.

4. Fill the next circle with solid black.

5. Fill the largest circle with paper and change the line to 2 pt. It will appear that you have selected the entire target.

6. With the largest circle selected, bring it to the front.

7. Send it to the back.

8. Select the third circle which is black, and send it to the back.

9. Select the largest circle, and send it to the back.

10. Save the publication as **RE5-1.**

11. Print the publication and close it.

Review Exercise 5–2

1. Open **TRUCK** from the *GRAPHICS* directory.

2. Move the objects on the page to look like Figure 5–9.

3. Fill the shapes with the fills shown.

4. Copy and paste or draw any missing shapes.

5. Save the publication as **RE5-2.**

6. Print the publication and close it.

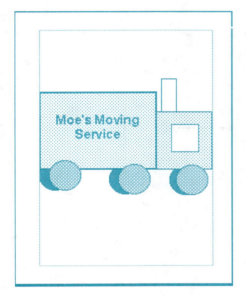

Figure 5–9
You can use the tools and skills you have learned to create this illustration.

Review Exercise 5-3

1. Create the publication shown in Figure 5–10 using the rectangle tool, ellipse tool, line tool, text tool, and ruler guides.

2. Save the publication as **RE5-3.**

3. Print the publication and end your PageMaker session.

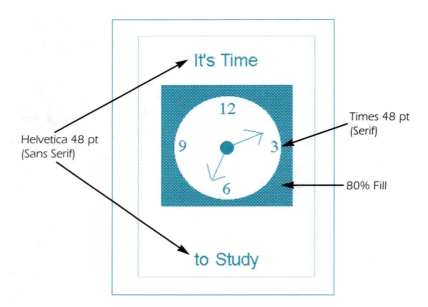

Figure 5–10
You can draw circles and ovals with the ellipse tool.

Helvetica 48 pt
(Sans Serif)

It's Time

12

9   3

6

to Study

Times 48 pt
(Serif)

80% Fill

Advanced Graphics

OBJECTIVES

After completing this lesson, you will be able to:

1. Use the Control palette.
2. Crop objects.
3. Resize objects.
4. Rotate objects.
5. Reflect objects.
6. Skew objects.
7. Wrap text around a graphic.

Estimated Time: 1 hour

USING THE CONTROL PALETTE

The Control palette offers you many ways to handle both text and graphic objects. When you select an object and choose Control palette from the Window menu, the Control palette looks like Figure 6–1. It contains options for changing objects. When a text block or the text tool is selected, the Control palette contains options for manipulating text. If nothing is selected, the Control palette displays only the location of the pointer arrow. For now, you will learn about using the Control palette to manipulate graphic objects.

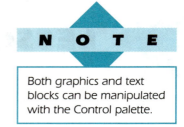

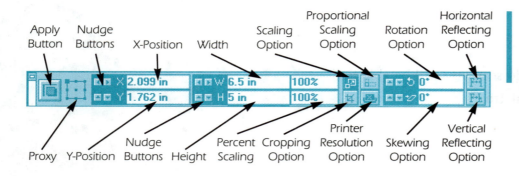

Figure 6–1
The Control palette allows you to modify graphic objects and text blocks.

To open the Control palette:

• Select an object.

• Choose **Control palette** from the **Window** menu.

To Close the Control palette:

• Click the close box.

-or-

Choose **Control palette** from the **Window** menu.

Choosing a Reference Point

Before you can manipulate an object, you must choose a reference point. A reference point is the stationary part of an object that PageMaker will use when you make changes to the object. The reference point can be a corner, a point on the side of an object, or a point in the middle of the selected object. The Control palette Proxy, shown in Figure 6–1, shows where the reference point is on the selected object. Using the reference point, you can easily control the rotation, reflection, cropping, and resizing of an object. The location of the reference point can determine how the object will look after it is changed.

To set the reference point:

- Select the object.
- Click one of its handles.

  -or-

  Click on a corner, side, top, bottom, or center on the **Proxy.**

Nudge Buttons

The nudge buttons are used to make small incremental changes to an object's location, size, or rotation. As shown in Figure 6–1, nudge buttons are located next to these options on the Control palette. You can change the location or size in increments of .01 inch or change the rotation in increments of 0.1 degree. After you click a nudge button, the Control palette displays the new value.

To change the location or size using the nudge buttons:

- Select the object.
- Click the appropriate nudge button to change the location or size by .01 inch at a time.

To change the angle of rotation using the nudge buttons:

- Select the object.
- Click the appropriate nudge button to change the angle 0.1 degree at a time.

N O T E

Sometimes a different nudge distance is needed. The default nudge can be changed in the Preferences dialog box.

Apply Button

The Apply button, shown in Figure 6–1, is used to record changes made on the Control palette. The figure that appears depends on the object that is selected. Pressing Enter or Return also activates the Apply button.

TRANSFORMING OBJECTS

PageMaker gives you control over objects in several ways. You can rotate them around a point, skew them by changing their angle, reflect them by changing their orientation, change their size, or remove part of the object by cropping. Cropping, rotating, and resizing can be done both manually and by using the Control palette. Reflecting and skewing can only be accomplished using the Control palette.

Cropping

Cropping an object allows you to cut off part of it. You can crop using the Control palette or using the cropping tool shown in Figure 6–2. Only imported graphics can be cropped. Figures created within Page-Maker must be modified using the tools you used to create the figure.

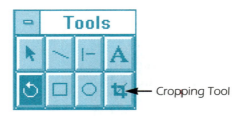

Cropping Tool

Figure 6–2
The cropping tool lets you remove part of a graphic; however, the original object will actually be unchanged in the computer's memory. At any time, you can uncrop the object to recover the area removed.

To crop an object using the Control palette:

• Select the object with the pointer tool.

• Select a reference point along the side to be cropped.

• Select the cropping option.

• Key the new height or width.

• Click the **Apply** button.

    -or-

    Press **Enter** or **Return.**

To crop an object manually:

• Select the object with the cropping tool.

• Select the handle on the side you wish to crop with the cropping tool.

• Crop the area you wish to remove by moving the handle toward the object.

N O T E

If you crop a graphic and then change your mind, you use the same cropping tool to replace the part removed. To do this, pull out the handle along the side that was cropped.

1. Open **GOAL** from the *GRAPHICS* directory.

2. Select the cropping tool and then the graphic.

3. Select a graphic handle on the bottom and crop away *Easy Goals.*

4. Choose **Control palette** from the **Window** menu.

5. Select the cropping option.

6. Select a top reference point on the Proxy.

7. Key **2.85 in** for the new height.

8. Click the **Apply** button.

9. Move the goal back to the corner.

EXERCISE 6–1

10. Save the publication as **EX6-1.**

11. Print the publication and leave it open for the next exercise.

Resizing

While working with publications, you may need to resize objects. You can resize an object manually using the pointer tool or the Control palette. The Control palette allows you more precision.

If you resize manually, you can maintain the proportions of an object by holding down the Shift key while changing the size of the object. If you use the Control palette, select the proportional-scaling option shown in Figure 6–1 to maintain the proportions. Maintaining the proportions will prevent distortion of your graphic. You can change just the length or the width of an object by turning off the proportional-scaling option; however, this will result in a distorted graphic.

To resize an object using the Control palette:

• Select the object.

• Select the proportional-scaling option from the Control palette if you wish to maintain proportions.

• Key a new width or height.

 -or-

 Key a new size percentage.

• Click the **Apply** button.

 -or-

 Press **Enter** or **Return.**

To resize an object manually:

• Select the object with the pointer tool.

• Click on a handle.

• Change the size of the object by dragging the object's handle in or out. If you wish to maintain the proportions of the object, hold down the **Shift** key while changing the object's size.

1. Click on the graphic. Select the handle on the lower-right corner with the pointer tool.

2. Enlarge the object proportionally by dragging so it is approximately 1 inch wider and 1 inch longer.

3. Copy the graphic and paste the new object in the lower-right corner.

4. Key in **75%** for the new width of the new graphic.

N O T E

You can move the Control palette by grabbing it along the left margin and placing it in a new location.

EXERCISE 6–2

5. On the Control palette, select the proportional-scaling option.

6. Save the publication as **EX6-2.**

7. Print the publication and leave it open for the next exercise.

Rotating

To spice up your publications, you may want to rotate graphics. On the Control palette, the rotating value is in degrees, as shown in Figure 6–1. PageMaker lets you rotate objects as much as 360 degrees. When you want to rotate an object, simply change the rotating value. You can also rotate an object manually using the rotating tool in the Toolbox as shown in Figure 6–3.

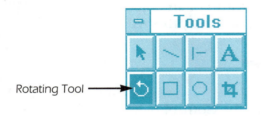

Rotating Tool

To rotate an object using the Control palette:

• Select the object.

• Select a reference point.

• Key a new rotation value.

• Click the **Apply** button.

-or-

Press **Enter** or **Return.**

To rotate an object manually:

• Select the rotating tool.

• Select a reference point by clicking on a handle with the starburst.

• Drag the starburst away from the reference point. A box and a rotation lever will appear to use as a guide for your new placement. If you do not drag the starburst away, only a lever will appear attached to the actual figure.

• Choose the new position of the object.

1. Select **rotating tool** on the Toolbox.

2. Click on the original graphic, which is located in the upper-left corner.

3. Click on the bottom-right handle and rotate the handle counterclockwise toward the top.

EXERCISE 6-3

4. Your object should be rotated as shown in Figure 6–4, although the position may be slightly different.

5. Using the Control palette, change the rotation of the graphic to **45 degrees.**

6. Using the pointer tool, move the graphic into the left-top corner of the page.

7. Save the publication as **EX6-3.**

8. Print the publication and leave it open for the next exercise.

Figure 6–4
Rotating the handle upward swings the object from that point.

Reflecting

Reflecting an object allows you to change the orientation of the graphic as shown in Figure 6–1. The object can be flipped vertically or horizontally. The Control palette provides both options using figures to demonstrate the position.

To reflect an object:

• Select the object with the pointer tool.

• Select the appropriate reflecting option on the Control palette.

1. Select the smaller graphic in the lower-right corner. Copy it and paste the new one in the lower-left corner.

EXERCISE 6-4

2. Using the Control palette's reflecting option, flip the new graphic **right to left** and then **up to down.**

3. Move the graphic back to the lower-left corner.

4. Save the publication as **EX6-4.**

5. Print the publication and leave it open for the next exercise.

Skewing

When you want to create an unusual special effect, you can skew an object by keying in a skew angle in the skewing option on the Control palette, as shown in Figure 6–1.

To skew an object:

• Select the object with the pointer tool.

• Select a reference point.

• Key a skew angle in the skewing option on the Control palette.

• Click the **Apply** button.

   -or-

   Press **Enter** or **Return.**

1. Select the graphic in the lower-right corner. Copy it and paste the new one in the center of the page.

2. Using the skewing option on the Control palette, change the skewing of the new graphic to **15 degrees.**

3. Save the publication as **EX6-5.**

4. Print the publication and close it.

WRAPPING TEXT AROUND OBJECTS

In a previous chapter you added an inline graphic to a text block. Another way to add interest to text is to place a graphic so that the text flows around the object. To do this, use the Text wrap command, as shown in Figure 6–5.

Text can flow over, around, or beside an object when the Wrap option is used. Text can also be arranged to stop at the top of the graphic, to flow across the top and bottom, or to flow on all four sides using the text flow option. The Standoff measurement determines the amount of white space around a graphic.

Once a graphic and the Text wrap option have been selected, a second boundary in the form of a dotted line will appear around the graphic, as shown in Figure 6–5. Handles will appear at each of the four corners. You can use these handles to customize the flow of text around the graphic by moving the boundary lines. You can also create additional handles on the boundaries by clicking anywhere along a boundary. The new handles allow you to customize the angle of the line.

N O T E

You can undo any changes you have made to an object using the Control palette by rekeying the original value or clicking on the reflecting buttons. If you are unsure how the changed object will look, record the original value so that you can return to it easily. You can also use the Undo command under the Edit menu or Remove transformation under the Element menu to undo changes.

EXERCISE 6–5

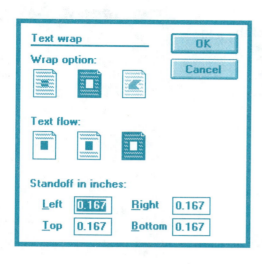

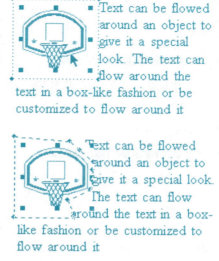

To wrap text around a graphic:

• Select the object with the pointer tool.

• Choose **Text wrap** from the **Element** window.

• Select the **Wrap** option that you wish.

• Select the **Text flow** option that you wish.

• Select the **Standoff measurement** that you wish.

• Click **OK.**

To customize the text wrap boundaries:

• Select the object with the pointer tool.

• Click on a handle at one of the four corners of the dotted line.

• Move the boundary.

To add handles to the text wrap boundaries:

• Select the object with the pointer tool.

• Click on the dotted line to create a new handle.

• Move the boundary.

To remove text wrap from a graphic:

• Select the object with the pointer tool.

• Choose **Text wrap** from the **Element** window.

• Select the new **Wrap** option that you wish.

• Select the new **Text flow** option that you wish.

• Click **OK.**

1. Open the file **FNDRAISE** from the *GRAPHICS* directory.

2. Move the graphic on the pasteboard to the top-left corner of the page so that it covers the word *FUN*.

3. Choose **Text wrap** from the **Element** window.

4. Click on the middle Wrap option. Use the default standoff setting.

5. Click **OK.**

6. Save the publication as **EX6-6.**

7. Print the publication and end your PageMaker session.

TRUE/FALSE

In the blank space before each sentence, place a **T** if the statement is true and an **F** if it is false.

_____ 1. The Control palette uses the Proxy to determine the size of an object.

_____ 2. Nudge buttons are used to change the rotation of an object.

_____ 3. The Apply button can be accessed by pressing Return or Enter.

_____ 4. You can use the reflecting tool to change the orientation of an object.

_____ 5. When you wrap text around an object, the text can only flow to the right of the text.

COMPLETION

Fill in the blank.

6. Explain how the Proxy establishes a reference point.

_____

_____

7. What two ways can you crop an object?

_____

_____

8. What does the rotating tool do?

_____

_____

9. When would you skew an object?

_____

_____

10. What purpose does the standoff value serve in text wrap?

_____

_____

REVIEW EXERCISE 6–1

1. Open **OVERVIEW** from the *GRAPHICS* directory.
2. Crop the computer so the printer and all extra white space is deleted.
3. Resize the graphic to 125%, maintaining its proportions.
4. Flip the computer right to left.
5. Place the graphic in the lower-left corner of the page, wrapping the text around it.
6. Change the boundaries to wrap the text more tightly on the right side.
7. Save the publication as **RE6-1.**
8. Print the publication and close it.

REVIEW EXERCISE 6–2

1. Open **PRINTERS** from the *GRAPHICS* directory.
2. Create the publication shown in Figure 6–6 using the Control palette.
3. Copy and paste the title graphic as often as necessary.
4. You will need to rotate the title graphic 25 degrees, reduce it to 50%, and wrap text using a .1 standoff.
5. Save the publication as **RE6-2.**
6. Print the publication and close the publication.

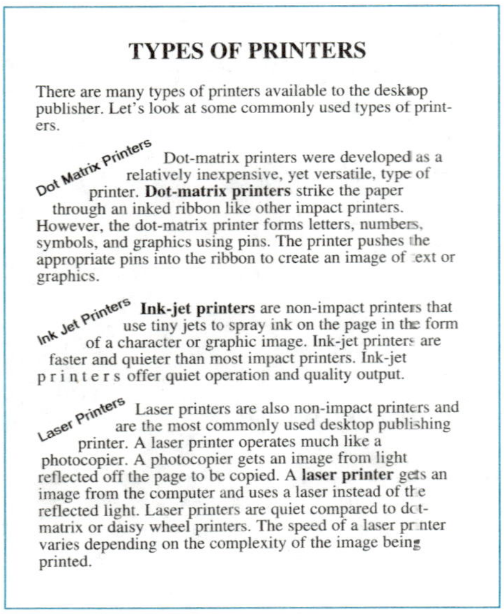

TYPES OF PRINTERS

There are many types of printers available to the desktop publisher. Let's look at some commonly used types of printers.

Dot Matrix Printers Dot-matrix printers were developed as a relatively inexpensive, yet versatile, type of printer. **Dot-matrix printers** strike the paper through an inked ribbon like other impact printers. However, the dot-matrix printer forms letters, numbers, symbols, and graphics using pins. The printer pushes the appropriate pins into the ribbon to create an image of text or graphics.

Ink Jet Printers **Ink-jet printers** are non-impact printers that use tiny jets to spray ink on the page in the form of a character or graphic image. Ink-jet printers are faster and quieter than most impact printers. Ink-jet p r i n t e r s offer quiet operation and quality output.

Laser Printers Laser printers are also non-impact printers and are the most commonly used desktop publishing printer. A laser printer operates much like a photocopier. A photocopier gets an image from light reflected off the page to be copied. A **laser printer** gets an image from the computer and uses a laser instead of the reflected light. Laser printers are quiet compared to dot-matrix or daisy wheel printers. The speed of a laser printer varies depending on the complexity of the image being printed.

Figure 6–6
You can use text as well as a graphic as an object.

LESSON 7

Layout

OBJECTIVES

After completing this lesson, you will be able to:

1. Create appealing layouts.
2. Set up a new layout.
3. Insert and remove pages.
4. Set columns.
5. Flow text into columns.

Estimated Time: 1 hour

CREATING AN APPEALING PAGE LAYOUT

Desktop publishing can be complex. To simplify the process, you should determine the page layout before adding text or graphics. A page layout is a plan or set of guidelines for a page. Paper size, page orientation, number of pages, margin settings, columns, and the arrangement of columns on a page make up the page layout.

The main objectives of a layout are readability and visual appeal. A publication with a well-designed page layout, such as the one shown in Figure 7–1, can motivate the reader and keep the reader's interest. The following guidelines will help you create an appealing layout:

- Create asymmetrical layouts when possible, meaning that objects do not mirror each other on each side of the page.

- Enliven a publication with graphics that relate to the text.

- Be generous with the use of white space, which is the area on a page that remains blank.

- Use fonts creatively to make the publication more visually exciting, but don't overdo it. Limit yourself to two or three typefaces.

- Use boldface, italic, and underlining sparingly.

Figure 7–1
A well designed newsletter makes use of a multicolumn layout and white space to draw attention to the articles.

SETTING UP A NEW LAYOUT

Layout decisions begin at the Page setup dialog box, which appears after you choose New from the File menu. Here you will select page size, page orientation, starting page number, number of pages, and margins. See Figure 7–2 for locations of these options.

N O T E

Once a publication has been created, you can change the Page setup at any time by choosing Page setup from the File menu.

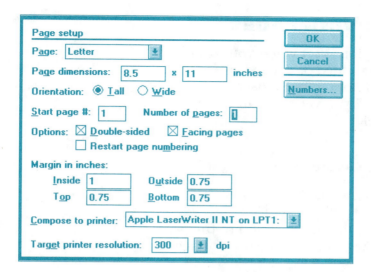

Page setup

Page: Letter ▼

Page dimensions: 8.5 × 11 inches   OK   Cancel   Numbers...

Orientation: ⦿ Tall ◯ Wide

Start page #: 1   Number of pages: 1

Options: ☒ Double-sided   ☒ Facing pages
☐ Restart page numbering

Margin in inches:
Inside 1   Outside 0.75
Top 0.75   Bottom 0.75

Compose to printer: Apple LaserWriter II NT on LPT1: ▼

Target printer resolution: 300 ▼ dpi

Figure 7–2
The Page setup dialog box is your first step in the decision-making process needed to make an attractive layout.

N O T E

Tall orientation is sometimes referred to as portrait. Wide is sometimes called landscape orientation.

N O T E

If you have a layout of only two pages, choosing page 2 as the starting page and selecting Double-sided and Facing pages will ensure that you can see both pages at the same time.

N O T E

Tabloid-size paper is also called ledger paper. Letter-half and Legal half sizes are half the size of letter and legal paper. These sizes can be used for creating a folded booklet.

▶ **EXERCISE 7–1**

You can select either Tall or Wide as the orientation of a publication. Orientation is the vertical or horizontal position of the page.

To view pages that will face each other when printed, you can choose Double-sided and Facing pages in the Page setup dialog box. This helps you choose a layout that is attractive for the reader, who will see the open pages as a single unit.

Among the most common page sizes to choose from are letter, legal, and tabloid. A standard sheet of paper commonly used for letters measures 8.5 × 11 inches, while the size of legal paper is 8.5 × 14 inches. Tabloid paper is 11 × 14 inches. You can also create a custom page size by keying in specific page dimensions.

To set up a new layout:

- Choose **New** from the **File** menu. The Page setup dialog box appears.

- Select the appropriate layout options.

- Choose **OK** to accept the new settings. An empty page appears.

1. Create a new publication.

2. Change the page size to legal and the orientation to wide.

3. Change the start page number to 2 and the number of pages to 3.

4. Make sure the options are set for Double-sided and Facing pages.

5. Change the margins to 2 inches on the inside, outside, top, and bottom.

6. Click **OK.**

7. Save the publication as **EX7-1.**

8. Leave the publication open for the next exercise.

INSERTING AND REMOVING PAGES

The number of pages in a publication is set when you first create a new publication, but pages can be added or deleted as needed. If you delete, be careful that you do not remove a page that contains text or graphics you wish to keep. However, you can use the Undo or Restore command to return deleted pages.

To insert a new page:

- Select **Insert pages** from the **Layout** menu as shown in Figure 7–3.

- Key in the number of additional pages you need.

- Click on the button to indicate the new location of the pages. They may be placed before, after, or between current pages.

- Click **OK.**

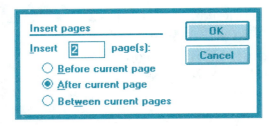

Figure 7–3
The Insert page dialog box automatically defaults to two pages.

To remove a page:

- Choose **Remove pages** from the **Layout** menu, as shown in Figure 7–4.

- Key in the beginning page number you wish to remove.

- Key in the ending page number you wish to remove. If you only want to remove a single page, the beginning and ending page numbers will be the same.

- Click **OK.**

Figure 7–4
The Remove dialog box defaults to the pages that are currently on the screen.

1. Insert three more pages into your publication before the current pages. Click **OK.** Since there is no text on the pages, it will appear that the pages have been entered after the current page.

2. Change the Page setup to letter size. Your margins will change to the default values.

► **EXERCISE 7–2**

3. Change the margins to 1 inch. Click **OK.**

4. Remove pages 4 to 7 from your publication. A dialog box will warn you that you will lose the contents of those pages. Click **OK.**

5. Save the publication as **EX7-2.**

6. Leave the publication open for the next exercise.

SETTING COLUMNS

PageMaker allows you to create publications with up to 20 columns per page. The width of each column and number of columns on a page work together to produce an effective publication.

To change the number of columns on a page:

- Choose **Column guides** from the **Layout** menu. The Column guides dialog box appears, as shown in Figure 7–5.

- Select the number of columns you want on a page.

- Key in the desired space between columns.

- If you have facing pages and want to set different columns for each page, click on **Set left and right pages separately.**

- Choose **OK.**

N O T E

You might want to limit the number of columns you use so there is enough space within each column to fit at least five words on a line.

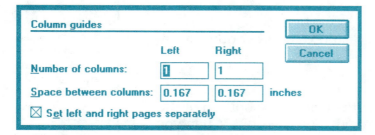

Figure 7–5
The Column guides dialog box uses 0.167 inch as the default space between columns. You can make your gutters wider to add more white space to your publication.

To change the width of a column:

- "Drag" the column guide with the pointer tool.

- Move the column guide to a new location to change the column width. Both guides representing the gutter will move at once.

1. Set the number of columns on the left and right separately.

2. Place 3 columns on the left page.

3. Set the width between columns at .5 inch.

4. Place 2 columns on the right page.

5. Set the width between columns at .5 inch.

6. On Page 3 make the left column smaller than the right column.

EXERCISE 7–3

7. Save the publication as **EX7-3.**

8. Leave the publication open for the next exercise.

FLOWING TEXT INTO COLUMNS

Once a layout has been set, text and graphics can be placed on the page. Text can be "poured" or *flowed* into columns manually, one column at a time, or continuously using the Autoflow command. Text that flows from one column to another is linked, so that any change in one column repositions the text in all linked columns.

To flow text into a single column:

- Choose **Place** from the **File** menu.

- Select the file you wish to import.

- Using the loaded cursor that appears, click inside the column into which you wish to flow the text. Text will flow down the column and stop at the bottom. If there is additional text, a down arrow will appear.

To flow text from one column into the next column:

- Using the pointer tool, click on the **down arrow** at the bottom of the column. A loaded cursor will appear in the form of a text icon.

- Click in the next column. Text will again flow down the column and stop. If there is additional text, another down arrow will appear.

To re-flow text within a column:

- Using the pointer tool, click on the icon at the bottom of the column and "drag" up until a single line is visible. When you release the mouse, the text will disappear and a down arrow will be visible.

- Click on the down arrow. A text icon will appear and the single line will disappear.

- Click in the column. Text will reflow down the column.

To flow text using the Autoflow command:

- Choose **Autoflow** from the **Layout** menu.

- Choose **Place** from the **File** menu.

- Select the file you wish to import.

- A loaded cursor will appear as the autoflow text icon. Click inside the first column into which you wish to flow the text. Text will flow down the column and continue on to each succeeding column. If additional pages are needed, the Autoflow command will create new pages until all text is placed.

Once text has been flowed into a column, the margins of the text block are set even if you change the width of the column. To change the width of the text block, you will have to use the handles of the text block to change its size or reflow the column.

It is not necessary to click exactly on the left margin of the column to have text fill the column. However, to ensure that the text flows from the top of the column, you must click at the top. If necessary, you may drag the text block to the top of the column after the text flows into the column.

To autoflow text from a column of text already placed:

- Choose **Autoflow** from the **Layout** menu.

- Using the pointer tool, click on the **down arrow** at the bottom of the column. An autoflow text icon will appear.

- Click in the next column. Text will flow down the column and continue on to each succeeding column.

1. **Place** the text file **FORMAT** from the *LAYOUT* directory. A loaded cursor appears.

► **EXERCISE 7–4**

2. Flow the text file into the first column on page 2. Continue until all the text is placed.

3. Make the size of the middle column on page 2 slightly smaller by moving one of the column guides. The text size will be unchanged.

4. Close up all the text except the first column.

5. Choose **Autoflow.**

6. Select the first column of text. Click on the **down arrow.** The loaded autoflow cursor will appear.

7. Reflow the text into the second column. It will flow until all the text is placed.

8. Save the publication as **EX7-4.**

9. Print the publication and close it.

TRUE/FALSE

In the blank space before each sentence, place a **T** if the statement
is true and an **F** if it is false.

_____ 1. The main objective of a good layout is to place as much
text on a page as possible.

_____ 2. Orientation of a page can be either vertical or horizontal.

_____ 3. The page setup cannot be changed once the new publication has appeared on the screen.

_____ 4. PageMaker limits to five the number of columns you
can place on a page.

_____ 5. When flowing text into a column, the loaded cursor
can be in the form of a text icon or an autoflow icon.

COMPLETION

Fill in the blank.

6. List at least two ways to add readability and visual appeal to a
layout.

_____

_____

7. What is the first step in designing a layout?

_____

_____

8. Why would you want to see facing pages?

_____

_____

9. What would happen if you removed a page that contained text
or graphics?

_____

_____

10. What is the purpose of the Autoflow option?

_____

_____

REVIEW EXERCISE 7–1

1. Open **INFOTECH** from the *LAYOUT* directory.

2. Use the material supplied to create a layout like the one shown in Figure 7–6. Text and graphics are on the pasteboard. You may need to move the pages over to see them.

3. Save the publication as **RE7-1.**

4. Print the publication and close it.

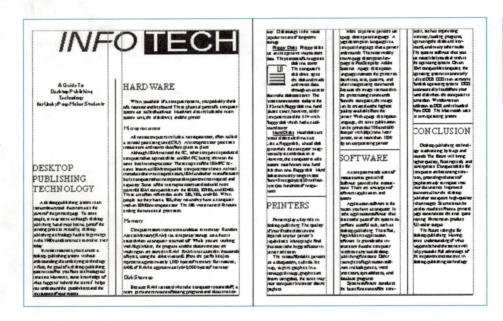

Figure 7–6
Informational brochures like INFOTECH are easier to read if they contain white space to rest the eye.

REVIEW EXERCISE 7–2

1. Open **POSTER** from the *LAYOUT* directory.

2. Use the text and any of the graphics supplied to create an attractive layout for a one-page informational poster. Change fonts, sizes, columns, or spacing whenever you feel it will improve readability. Use any of the skills you have previously learned.

3. Save the publication as **RE7-2.**

4. Print the publication and close it.

LESSON 8

Advanced Design

OBJECTIVES

After completing this lesson, you will be able to:

1. Use secondary margin guides.
2. Use ruler guides.
3. Use snap to guides.
4. Lock guides.
5. Change ruler settings.
6. Set automatic and hanging indents.
7. Set tabs.
8. Choose leaders.
9. Determine appropriate hyphenation.
10. Use paragraph specifications.

Estimated Time: 1 hour

PageMaker provides you with several ruler and guide options for use in the design process. In the previous lesson, you learned to use the column guides into which you flowed text. In this lesson you will use other guides, as well as rulers, to design your page.

USING MARGIN GUIDES

Previously you have set margins using the Page setup dialog box. In addition to using the dialog box, PageMaker gives you another set of vertical margin guides (see Figure 8–1) that can be pulled from the side page margins. Unlike Page setup margin guides that stay the same throughout the publication, these secondary margin guides can be different on each page.

Once the new margin guides are pulled into place, text will flow between them rather than between the original margins. Thus, you can set up margins in the Page setup dialog box, then use the secondary margin guides to change the margins on individual pages.

To create a secondary vertical or side margin guide:

- With the pointer tool, click on the vertical margin on the left or right side of the screen to "grab" a secondary margin.
- Drag away from the existing margin in either direction to move the secondary margin into position.

To remove a secondary vertical margin guide:

- With the pointer tool, "grab" the secondary margin.
- Drag the secondary margin back to the permanent margin or off the page.

1. Open **PALETTE** from the *DESIGN* directory.

2. Move the left secondary margin to the 4.25-inch mark.

3. Change the page view to **Actual size.** If needed, adjust the margin to the specified measurement.

4. Save the publication as **EX8-1.**

5. Leave the publication open for the next exercise.

USING RULER GUIDES

Ruler guides can help you design pages. As shown in Figure 8–1, ruler guides are lines that extend from the tick marks of the vertical and horizontal rulers. Like secondary margin guides, ruler guides can be different on each page. Unlike secondary margin guides, ruler guides are both vertical and horizontal. In addition, more than one ruler guide can appear on a single page.

N O T E

Notice that the side margins are a different color from the top margins. PageMaker frequently uses color changes to indicate alignment. Once you have pulled away the secondary margin, the side margin becomes the same color as the top. If you move the secondary margin back, the permanent margin will change color to indicate alignment.

EXERCISE 8–1

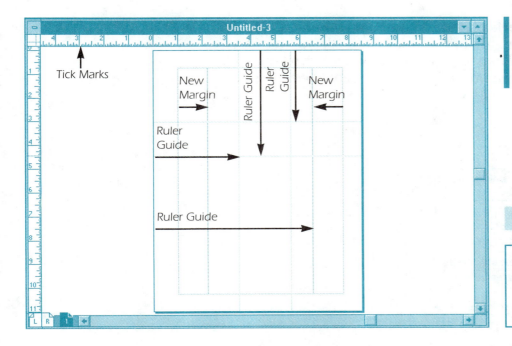

Figure 8–1
Secondary margin
guides and ruler guides
increase your layout
options.

N O T E

Tick marks are the division
lines on a ruler. Figure 8–1
shows tick marks on the
vertical and horizontal
rulers.

To create a vertical ruler guide:

- With the pointer tool, click on the vertical ruler on the left side of the screen to "grab" a guide.

- Drag away from the ruler to move the guide into position.

To create a horizontal ruler guide:

- With the pointer tool, click on the horizontal ruler at the top of the screen to "grab" a guide.

- Drag away from the ruler to move the guide into position.

N O T E

Ruler lines and guide lines
used in PageMaker are visible on the screen, but do
not appear on the printed
page.

▶ **EXERCISE 8–2**

1. Change the page view to **Fit in window.**

2. Using the vertical ruler, place guides at 1.5 inches and at 4 inches.

3. Using the horizontal ruler, place ruler guides at 1 inch and at 4 inches.

4. Change the page view to **Actual size.** If needed, adjust the guides to the specified measurements.

5. Save the publication as **EX8-2.**

6. Leave the publication open for the next exercise.

SELECTING SNAP TO GUIDES

The Snap to guides option under Guides and rulers, as shown in Figure 8–2, allows you to position text or graphics precisely by making alignment of objects easier. When the Snap to guides

N O T E

The Snap to rulers option
offers the same attributes
for rulers as Snap to guides
provides for margins.

option is selected, objects placed near margin and ruler guides will line up or snap to them. "Snap to guides" is the default or preset choice for PageMaker. Snap to guides is on when a checkmark appears beside the selection on the pull-down menu. Selecting the option "toggles" between on and off.

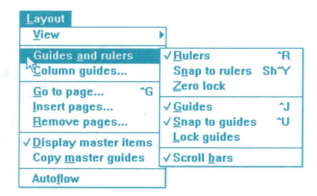

Figure 8–2
Use of Snap to guides speeds up placement and ensures more accurate positioning of objects.

Turning off Snap to guides allows you more freedom of movement when aligning text or graphics. Turn the option off if you want to place an object near the guide but not on it.

To turn on Snap to guides:

• Choose **Guides and rulers** from the **Layout** menu.

• Choose **Snap to guides.** You will see a checkmark next to the name.

To turn off Snap to guides:

• Choose **Guides and rulers** from the **Layout** menu.

• Choose **Snap to guides.** The checkmark will disappear.

LOCKING GUIDES

The Lock guides option under Guides and rulers allows you to lock a secondary margin or ruler guide into place. This is helpful if you want to make sure that the guide is not inadvertently moved during the layout process.

To lock guides:

• Choose **Guides and rulers** from the **Layout** menu.

• Choose **Lock guides.** A checkmark will be visible.

To unlock guides:

• Choose **Guides and rulers** from the **Layout** menu.

• Choose **Lock guides.** The checkmark will disappear.

1. Change the view to **Fit in Window.**

2. Make sure that Snap to guides is on.

3. Choose the **Zero lock.**

4. Place the palette graphic within the top rectangle formed by the ruler guides. The top-left corner will be at the 1.5-inch mark on horizontal and 1-inch mark on the vertical ruler.

5. Save the publication as **EX8-3.**

6. Leave the publication open for the next exercise.

▶ **EXERCISE 8–3**

CHANGING RULER SETTINGS

PageMaker allows you to change the ruler settings on both the horizontal and vertical rulers and then to lock those new settings in place. This is helpful when you wish to measure from a specific point, such as the center of the page.

As shown in Figure 8–3, in the upper-left corner of the publication page where the rulers meet there is a box with intersecting dotted lines. This box is called the zero-point marker. Using the pointer tool to grab these lines, you can move along the rulers. When you release the mouse button, the point at which you stopped will become the new zero point on the ruler.

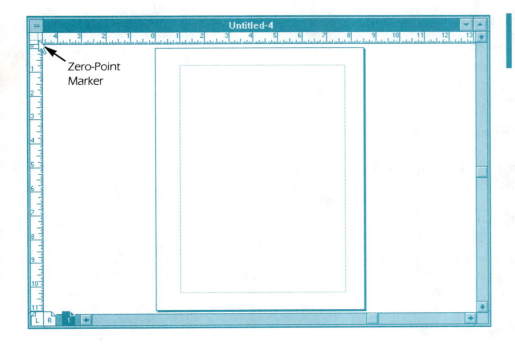

Zero-Point Marker

Figure 8–3
The zero-point marker lets you change the setting of the ruler.

If you move horizontally along the ruler, only the horizontal ruler is affected. Moving vertically will change the vertical ruler. Moving diagonally from the upper-left to the lower-right will change both rulers.

To change ruler settings:

• Grab the **zero-point marker.**

• Move the marker either horizontally, vertically, or diagonally to a new position.

Once a new ruler setting is in place, you can lock the setting by choosing the Zero lock option from Guides and rulers.

Using the Snap to rulers option ensures that an object will move to the nearest tick mark on the ruler.

The Guides and rulers menu offers an option to hide rulers and guides. If Guides is checkmarked, the guides will be visible. If Rulers is checkmarked, the rulers will be visible. Toggling to remove the checkmarks removes the rulers and guides from the screen. This is useful if you wish to see what your publication will look like without the distractions of nonprinting lines.

1. Move the zero-point marker to the intersection of the ruler guides at 1 inch on the vertical ruler and 1.5 inches on the horizontal ruler.

2. Make sure the Snap to rulers option is checked.

3. Lock the new ruler settings.

4. Save the publication as **EX8-4.**

5. Print the publication and leave it open for the next exercise.

SETTING INDENTS

The Indents/tabs option shown in Figure 8–4 allows you to make choices about the margins of a single paragraph. This option is found in the Type menu. On the left side above the ruler are two black triangles called indent icons. The top triangle controls the left margin of the first line of a paragraph. The bottom triangle controls the left margin of the remainder of the paragraph. A single triangle on the right controls the right margin of the whole paragraph.

Moving the top-left triangle toward the right will allow you to automatically indent the paragraph affected by this ruler. Moving the bottom triangle to the right will allow you to create hanging indents.

To create an automatic indent:

• Move the top-left triangle along the ruler to the location of the desired indent.

EXERCISE 8-4

N O T E

The Indents/tab ruler changes depending on the view you have chosen. If you are using Actual size, the ruler will be 5 inches wide and must be scrolled to see the tabs across the entire page. If you are using Fit in window, you will be able to see all the tabs.

N O T E

Changes in the Indents/tabs ruler affect only the paragraph in which the cursor is located unless additional paragraphs have been highlighted.

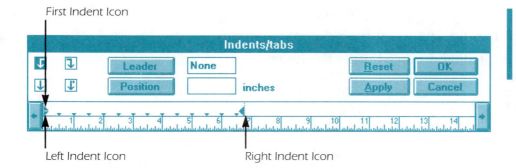

First Indent Icon

Indents/tabs

Leader None   Reset OK
Position   inches Apply Cancel

1 2 3 4 5 6 7 8 9 10 11 12 13 14

Left Indent Icon   Right Indent Icon

To create a hanging indent:

• Move the bottom-left triangle along the ruler to the location of the desired indent. The top triangle will move with it.

• Move the top-left triangle back to the left margin.

1. Flow the text located on the pasteboard into the right column of your publication between the left secondary margin and the permanent right margin.

2. Highlight the first paragraph.

3. Choose **Indents/tabs** from the **Type** menu.

4. Set the top triangle at the .25-inch mark. Click **OK.**

5. Highlight the rest of the text below the opening paragraph.

6. Choose **Indents/tabs.**

7. Set the bottom triangle at the .375-inch mark. If necessary, move the top triangle back to the left margin. Click **OK.**

8. Save the publication as **EX8-5.**

9. Print the publication and leave it open for the next exercise.

SETTING TABS

PageMaker presets a left tab every half-inch. To change the location or type of tab, use the Indents/tabs option from the Type menu.

As shown in Figure 8–5, the Indents/tabs ruler contains triangles indicating the positions of tabs. If you click on one of the preset tabs, all tabs to the left of the selected tab will be removed and an arrow will appear indicating the type of the new tab. Those to the right will remain unchanged. You may select a tab type either before or after clicking on a tab.

There are four types of tabs: left tabs, right tabs, center tabs, and decimal tabs. When a left tab is used, text is aligned at the tab stop using the left margin of the text. With a right tab, text is aligned at the tab stop using the right margin of the text. With a center tab,

EXERCISE 8–5

N O T E

Moving the bottom triangle will cause the top one to move also. To avoid this, you can position the bottom triangle first, and then move the top one to the desired location. However, you can also hold down the Shift key while dragging the bottom triangle to prevent the top triangle from moving.

N O T E

At least one tab on the ruler must show at all times. If all tabs are removed, PageMaker automatically resets the preset tabs at half-inch intervals.

text is aligned at the tab stop using the center of the text. When a decimal tab is used, numbers are aligned at their decimal points.

Tabs can be added, deleted, and moved using the Indents/tab ruler and the pointer tool. The Position button in Windows and the Position arrow in Macintosh (see Figure 8–5) can also be selected when you want to add, delete, move, or repeat tabs.

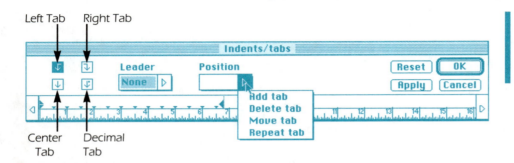

Figure 8–5
Clicking on the Position arrow will produce a menu of position choices.

To change a tab using the pointer tool:

- To add a tab, click on a new location on the Indents/tabs ruler.

- To remove a tab, select the tab and drag it off the Indents/tabs ruler. It will disappear.

- To move a tab, select the tab and drag it to the new location.

To change a tab using the Position button:

- To add a tab, key in a new location in the Position box, click on the **Position** button or arrow, and choose **Add tab.**

- To remove a tab, key into the Position box the location of the tab to be removed, click on the **Position** button or arrow, and choose **Delete tab.**

- To move a tab, select the tab to be moved, key in the new location in the Position box, click on the **Position** button or arrow, and choose **Move tab.**

- To repeat tabs at consistent intervals, select the second tab, click on the **Position** button or arrow, and choose **Repeat tab.** New tabs will appear at the same intervals as the first and second tab.

Another option that can be used in designing the look of a page is to select the Leader option from the Indents/tabs dialog box. The most frequently used leader is a series of periods used to draw the eye across the page to a tabbed item. To create a leader, click on a tab and then on the Leader button or arrow. A menu of choices will appear. Choose the one you want.

To place a leader before a tab:

- Click on the tab to be preceded by a leader.

- Click the **Leader** button.

- Select a leader style.

- Click **OK.**

- Tab to the new location. The leader will appear.

The Indents/tabs dialog box also has a button to reset the ruler to the preset half-inch interval tabs and a button to apply changes so that you can observe the effect on your work. If the dialog box prevents you from seeing your text, you can click on the title line with the pointer tool and drag the box to a better location.

▶ **EXERCISE 8–6**

1. Highlight the text below the opening paragraph.
2. Choose **Indents/tabs.**
3. Set a left tab at the .625-inch mark and a tab at the 1.25-inch mark.
4. Click **OK.**
5. Tab the second, fifth, eighth, and eleventh lines once.
6. Tab the third, sixth, ninth, and twelfth lines twice.
7. Save the publication as **EX8-6.**
8. Print the publication and leave it open for the next exercise.

CHOOSING HYPHENATION OPTIONS

In addition to using tabs, another way to change the look of a line is with hyphenation. Because of PageMaker's word-wrap feature, long words that wrap to the next line of text can leave a distracting gap on the line above. To remedy this situation, PageMaker automatically turns on the hyphenation option, as shown in the dialog box in Figure 8–6. However, if you do not wish to use the option, you can turn it off using the Hyphenation command in the Type menu. This is particularly important in publications such as posters and in headlines, where hyphens would not be appropriate.

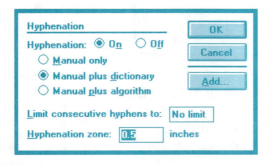

Figure 8–6
Besides turning hyphenation on and off, PageMaker also lets you choose to hyphenate manually or with a special dictionary.

To turn off hyphenation:

- Choose **Hyphenation** from the **Type** menu.

- Click **Off.**

- Click **OK.**

To turn on hyphenation:

- Choose **Hyphenation** from the **Type** menu.
- Click **On.**
- Click **OK.**

1. Select all of the text in your open publication.
2. Turn off all hyphenation.
3. Save the publication as **EX8**-**7.**
4. Print the publication and leave it open for the next exercise.

▶ **EXERCISE 8-7**

USING PARAGRAPH SPECIFICATIONS

A powerful design tool is the Paragraph specifications dialog box, shown in Figure 8–7. You have already used the Spacing button in this dialog box to set up kerning and leading choices. In addition, this tool allows you to choose with ease many other features that will add interest and readability to your publication. You can access the Paragraph specifications dialog box through the Type menu.

Paragraph specifications			OK
Indents:		**Paragraph space:**	Cancel
Left	0 inches	Before 0 inches	
First	0 inches	After 0 inches	Rules...
Right	0 inches		Spacing...

Alignment: Left   Dictionary: US English

Options:
- ☐ Keep lines together   ☐ Keep with next   0 lines
- ☐ Column break before   ☐ Widow control   0 lines
- ☐ Page break before   ☐ Orphan control   0 lines
- ☐ Include in table of contents

Figure 8–7
The Paragraph specifications dialog box allows you to make many choices at once without having to use individual commands.

N O T E

In PageMaker, a widow is a short line that falls at the bottom of a column or page. An orphan is a short line of a paragraph that falls at the top of a page. Both widows and orphans are undesirable because they seem to indicate lack of layout planning. Selecting Widow control and Orphan control in Paragraph specifications removes widows and orphans from your document.

Just as you can set the indents and margins of a paragraph using the Indents/tabs options, you can enter a number to set the left and right margins and indent the first line. In addition, just as you can set the alignment using the Alignment command, you can also select it here.

The amount of space between paragraphs can be set using the Before and After Paragraph space. In addition, as shown in Figure 8–8, using the Rules option you can place a rule line above or below a paragraph and choose the Line style.

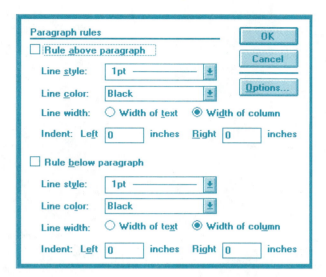

Figure 8–8
The Paragraph rules box offers you many choices, such as location, style, and width.

Other options allow you to choose how many lines to keep together when flowing text from one column or page to another and when to break a page or column.

1. Place the cursor in the first paragraph using the text tool.

2. Choose **Paragraph specifications.**

3. Using the Alignment button, choose **Right.** Click **OK.**

4. Choose **Guides and rulers.** Toggle **Guides** off.

5. Save the publication as **EX8-8.**

6. Print the publication and close it.

TRUE/FALSE

In the blank space before each sentence, place a **T** if the statement is true and an **F** if it is false.

_____ 1. Secondary margin guides can be different on every page.

_____ 2. You can only have one set of ruler guides on a page.

_____ 3. Snap to guides are useful to improve accuracy of placement of an object.

_____ 4. Zero-point markers remain the same in every publication.

_____ 5. An automatic indent is created using a triangle margin marker.

COMPLETION

Fill in the blank.

6. Why would you lock the guides of a publication?

_____

_____

7. What problem will you encounter when you make a hanging indent?

_____

_____

8. Explain the difference between the four types of tabs.

_____

_____

9. When would you turn off the hyphenation option?

_____

_____

10. What kinds of changes can you make using the Paragraph specifications box?

_____

_____

REVIEW EXERCISE 8–1

1. Open **MULTI** from the *DESIGN* directory.

2. Set the zero-point marker at the .75-inch page margins.

3. Make sure Snap to guides is on.

4. Move the secondary margins to 1-inch and 6-inch marks.

5. Using the horizontal ruler guides, place guides at the 6.25-, 6-, 1.75-, and 1.5-inch marks.

6. Using the vertical ruler guides, place guides at the 4.75-, 4.5-, 2.5-, and 2.25-inch marks.

7. Lock the guides.

8. Flow the text into areas designated in Figure 8–9. You will have to drag the shades up, reflow text, and adjust margins as needed. It is not important at this time where your lines break as long as you fill each area as designated.

9. Flow the major headline into the center grid, as designated in Figure 8–9.

10. Turn off hyphenation in the major headline.

11. Center the text of the major headline.

12. Using the **Rules option** from the Paragraph specifications, place a 2-point black rule above the major headline and one below it.

13. Use the **Rules option** to place the rule .5 inch above the text and .3 inch below the text.

14. Save the publication as **RE8-1.**

15. Print the publication and leave it open for the next exercise.

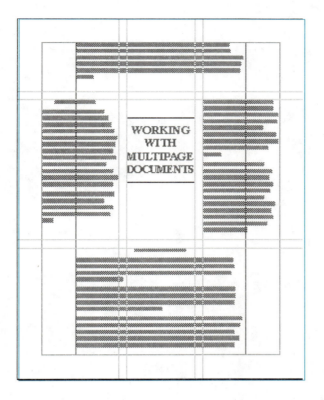

Figure 8–9
Using PageMaker tools and commands, you can create a publication that is interesting and easy to produce.

REVIEW EXERCISE 8–2

1. Highlight all of the text other than the title. Using Paragraph specifications, set a space of 0.1 inch after each paragraph.

2. Using the text tool, select the paragraph that begins with the words *Saddle Stitching* in bold. Use Paragraph specifications to set a column break before the paragraph.

3. Using the text tool, select the title *Types of Binding*. Use Paragraph specifications to place the title with the next 3 lines.

4. Set a center tab at 1 inch with a leader and a left tab at 2 inches with a leader. Click **OK.**

5. Tab from the right of the title and then from the left of the title to show the leaders.

6. Select the title *Planning the Margins*. Set a center tab at 2.5 with a leader and a left tab at 4.75 with a leader. Click **OK.**

7. Tab from the left of the title and then from the right of the title to show the leaders.

8. Save the publication as **RE8-2.**

9. Print the publication and close it.

LESSON 9

Shortcuts

OBJECTIVES

After completing this lesson, you will be able to:

1. Use master pages.
2. Use the Control palette for text.
3. Define and apply styles.
4. Use the Control palette for paragraphs.
5. Set up a Library palette.
6. Use the Color palette.

Estimated Time: 1 hour

USING MASTER PAGES

Using master pages can be a real time-saver when you want to create publications that contain recurring layouts, text, or graphics. Master page icons are located to the left of the actual page icons that appear at the bottom of your page when a file is open (see Figure 9–1). Clicking on master page icons lets you see one or two pages, depending on your Page setup choice of Double-sided Facing pages or Single pages.

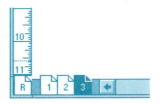 

Figure 9–1
Master page icons are labeled R if Double-sided pages is not selected. The icons are labeled L and R if the Double-sided option has been chosen in the Page setup.

Master pages are used to create headers and footers and to number pages automatically. Headers and footers are information blocks that can appear at the tops and bottoms of pages. They may include the name of the publication, the date, the section title, and the page number.

To number pages automatically, press Ctrl + Shift + 3 (Windows) or Command + Option + P (Macintosh). A page number marker LM (left page marker) or RM (right page marker) will appear. The markers can be read when your view of the page is enlarged. When you return to your actual pages, the numbers on the pages will match the numbers of the page icons.

Imported graphics and figures drawn in PageMaker, as well as text blocks, can be added to master pages. Once you have chosen elements for your master pages, by default these choices will be displayed on all of your actual pages. If you do not want to include master items on a page, choose Display master items from the Layout menu to toggle the selection off. The master items will disappear and will not be printed.

You can set columns, ruler guides, and secondary margins on master pages. The guides and columns you establish for the master pages will automatically appear on your actual pages unless you change them on the actual pages by using Column guides from the Layout menu or by moving the guides on the page.

If you make a change to a page, you can return to the guides and columns used on the master pages by choosing Copy master guides from the Layout menu. Your changes to the page will be replaced by the master page choices.

N O T E

It is easy to forget that you are on a master page. Check the icons to verify that you are in the location you need to be.

To add elements to a master page:

- Click on a **master page** icon.

- Choose the appropriate column guides.

- Set any ruler guides or secondary margins.

- Add headers or footers by creating text blocks with the necessary information.

- Add page numbers using **Ctrl + Shift + 3** (Windows) or **Command + Option + P** (Macintosh).

- Add any recurring text or graphics to the pages.

- Click on the **actual page** icon to return to the document.

N O T E

Notice the direction of the turn-down notches on both master page icons and actual page icons, as shown in Figure 9–1. When the Double-sided option is selected, there are two master pages. The right master page affects all odd-numbered pages. The left master page affects all even-numbered pages.

► EXERCISE 9–1

1. From the template directory *SHORTCUT*, open **MEMO.**

2. Click on the **master page** icon.

3. Choose **Column guides** from the **Layout** menu. Select **two** columns with the space between at .3 inch. Click **OK.**

4. Move the column guide so the left side of the guide is at the 3-inch mark.

5. Pull down a horizontal ruler guide to the 3-inch mark.

6. With the text tool, key **Copper H.S. Memo.** You may create a text block anywhere on the page.

7. Tab once. Key in **Page** and an automatic page number.

8. Place the text block below the bottom page margin and drag the block so it is as wide as the page margins. It is now a footer.

9. Choose **page 1.**

10. Save the publication as **EX9-1.**

11. Leave the publication open for the next exercise.

USING THE CONTROL PALETTE FOR TEXT

You have previously used the Control palette to modify graphics. It can also be used to modify text. Selecting text with the text tool will activate the text Control palette, shown in Figure 9–2, allowing you to change most text attributes quickly.

N O T E

If you are in the story editor, the Control palette will automatically open to the text or paragraph palette.

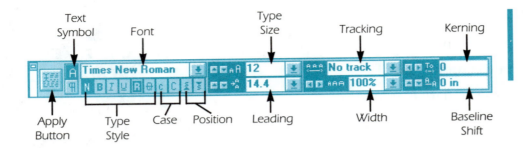

Text Symbol — Font — Type Size — Tracking — Kerning

Apply Button — Type Style — Case — Position — Leading — Width — Baseline Shift

Figure 9–2
With text selected, the Control palette can be used to change most text attributes.

The Control palette can be used to change fonts, size, tracking, kerning, style, case, position, leading, width, and baseline.

To change text using the Control palette:

- Highlight the text to be changed.

- Choose the **Control palette** from the **Window** menu.

- Select the **Text** button.

- Select the appropriate text attribute.

N O T E

The Control palette can be moved by dragging it from the left side.

1. Return to the **master page** icon.

2. Open the **Control palette.**

3. With the text tool, highlight all the text in the footer.

4. Change the size of the text to 9 point.

5. Change the font to a sans serif font such as Helvetica or Ariel.

6. Change the width to 120%.

7. Save the publication as **EX9-2.**

8. Leave the publication open for the next exercise.

EXERCISE 9–2

DEFINING AND APPLYING STYLES

Defining and then applying styles is a powerful shortcut in Page-Maker. Any type or paragraph choice you make to an individual paragraph can be applied to any other paragraph by using the Define styles option from the Type menu.

N O T E

In PageMaker, a paragraph is created whenever you press Return or Enter.

When you select the Define styles option, a dialog box similar to the one shown in Figure 9–3 will appear. It will give you a list of already-defined styles and the choice of modifying existing styles or creating new ones. Once you have chosen New or Edit, an Edit style dialog box, as shown in Figure 9–4, allows you to choose what style to base the text on and what the text following should be based on. You can also determine attributes such as type specifications, paragraph specifications, indents/tabs, and hyphenation for each style.

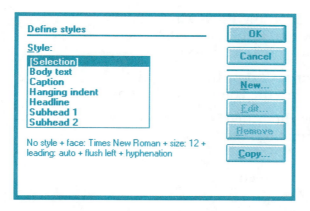

Figure 9–3
Defining styles lists all available styles such as Body text and Caption, as well as the specifications for each.

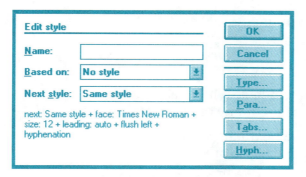

Figure 9–4
Using Styles can improve the look of your publication by making it more consistent.

Once a style has been defined, you can apply it to any paragraph using either the Style option from the Type menu or the Style palette from the Window menu. The advantage of using Styles is that once a body of text has been assigned a style, you can automatically change any part of the style, and all the text assigned that style will change.

To define a new style:

- Choose **Define styles** from the **Type** menu.

- Choose **New.**

- Assign a name to the style. It will be helpful to choose one that determines the use of the style, such as First-level heading.

- Determine if you wish the style to be similar to one already in the list of available styles. If it will be, click on the **Based on** button and choose the name of the style.

- Determine if you want the next paragraph to be based on a style already created. If so, click on the **Next style** button and choose the style name to follow.

- Assign type specifications by choosing **Type.** Choose the appropriate type. Click **OK** to return to the Edit style dialog box.

- Assign paragraph specifications by choosing **Para.** Choose the appropriate specification. Click **OK** to return to the Edit style dialog box.

- Assign indents/tabs by choosing **Tabs.** Choose the appropriate tabs and indents. Click **OK** to return to the Edit style dialog box.

- Determine hyphenation choices by choosing **Hyph.** Choose the appropriate hyphenation information. Click **OK** to return to the Edit style dialog box.

- Click **OK** to return to the publication screen.

To modify an existing style:

- Choose **Define styles** from the **Type** menu.

- Select the style you wish to modify.

- Choose **Edit.**

- If you wish to change the name on which a style is based, click on the **Based on** button and choose the name of another style.

- If you wish to change the style of the next paragraph, click on the **Next style** button and choose the name of another style.

- Assign type specifications by choosing **Type.** Choose the appropriate type. Click **OK** to return to the Edit style dialog box.

- Assign paragraph specifications by choosing **Para.** Choose the appropriate specification. Click **OK** to return to the Edit style dialog box.

- Assign indents/tabs by choosing **Tabs.** Choose the appropriate tabs and indents. Click **OK** to return to the Edit style dialog box.

- Determine hyphenation choices by choosing **Hyph.** Choose the appropriate hyphenation information. Click **OK** to return to the Edit style dialog box.

- Click **OK** to return to the publication screen.

To apply a style:

- Using the text tool, click on some part of the text of the paragraph to which you wish to apply the style.

- Choose **Styles** from the **Type** menu.

  -or-

  Choose **Style palette** from the **Window** menu.

- Choose the style you wish to apply to that paragraph.

Styles apply to paragraphs rather than individual words, so clicking anywhere on a text paragraph will allow you to assign a style to the complete paragraph.

1. Make sure you are on a master page. Move the text on the pasteboard that begins with the word *Date:* into the upper-right corner of the page. It should be placed between the column guide and the right margin guides. Drag the text block handle to fill the space.

2. Move the text on the pasteboard that begins with the word *To* into the lower-left corner of the page. It should be placed below the horizontal ruler and between the left margin and the column guide. Drag the text block handle to fill the space.

3. Choose **Define styles** from the **Type** menu.

4. Create a new style.

5. Name the new style **Memo Form.**

6. From the Type option, change the type size to **24-point bold**. Click **OK.**

7. From the Paragraph option, change the text to **Left alignment.** Click **OK** to return to Edit style and **OK** to return to Define styles.

8. Create another new style called **Memo Text.** Base it on Memo Form.

9. From the Type option, change the type style to **Normal.**

10. From the Paragraph option, change the text to **Right alignment.** Click **OK** to return to Edit style and **OK** to return to Define styles. Click **OK** to return to the page.

11. Select the top text block with the text tool. Choose **Style** from the **Type** menu and apply the **Memo Form** style.

12. Highlight the lower text block with the text tool.

13. Open the **Style palette.** Apply the **Memo Form** style to the lower text block.

14. Save the publication as **EX9-3.**

15. Leave the publication open for the next exercise.

USING THE CONTROL PALETTE FOR PARAGRAPHS

Another way to change the attributes of a paragraph is with the Control palette, as shown in Figure 9–5. Just as you used this palette to modify text attributes, you can modify paragraphs by clicking on a text block with the text tool and selecting the Paragraph symbol. The palette changes from a text palette to a paragraph palette.

The Control palette, with the Paragraph symbol selected, can change information about styles, the insertion point position, indentations, spaces before and after the paragraph, grid options, and alignment.

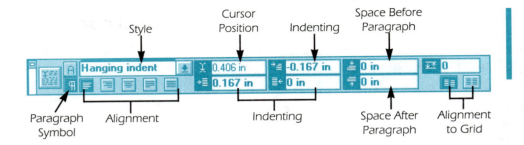

Style

Cursor
Position

Indenting

Space Before
Paragraph

Paragraph
Symbol

Alignment

Indenting

Space After
Paragraph

Alignment
to Grid

To change a paragraph attribute using the Control palette:
- Click on a paragraph with the text tool.
- Choose the **Control palette** from the **Window** menu.
- Click on the **Paragraph** symbol.
- **No style** should be selected in the Paragraph-style window.
- Change the appropriate attribute.

To apply a style using the Control palette:
- Click on a paragraph with the text tool.
- Choose the **Control palette** from the **Window** menu.
- Click on the **Paragraph** symbol.
- Pull down the list of styles and choose the appropriate one.
- Your paragraph will be assigned that style.

To modify a style using the Control palette:
- Click on a paragraph with the text tool.
- Choose the **Control palette** from the **Window** menu.
- Click on the **Paragraph** symbol.
- Pull down the list of styles and choose the appropriate one.
- Make changes to the Control palette. Only the selected body of text will be changed. A plus sign will appear next to the style to indicate a deviation from the original style.

To close a Control palette:
- Click on the close box located in the upper-left corner of the palette.

EXERCISE 9–4

1. Select the footer with the text tool.
2. Choose the **Control palette.** Select the **Paragraph** symbol.
3. With **No style** selected, change the alignment to **Right.**
4. Select the lower text block. The Control palette will change to Memo form style.

5. Change alignment to **Right.** Notice the plus sign that appears. Change the alignment back to **Left.**

6. Close the Style palette and the Control palette.

7. Save the publication as **EX9-4.**

8. Leave the publication open for the next exercise.

SETTING UP A LIBRARY PALETTE

A Library palette, as shown in Figure 9–6, is another shortcut that gives power to PageMaker. It allows you to store graphics and text for any publication, making the recall easy and fast.

Figure 9–6
The Library palette is an easy way to save frequently used graphics or text.

To set up a Library palette the first time:

- Choose **Library palette** from the **Window** menu.

- A directory dialog box will appear. Give the palette a name and save it to the appropriate location by using the directories.

- In *Windows,* a dialog box will appear, warning you that no such palette exists. It asks you if you want to create a new palette. Click **Yes.**

To open another Library palette:

- Choose **Library palette** from the **Window** menu. The most recent palette will appear.

- To use another palette, choose **Options** and then choose **Open library.** Locate the other palette.

- Select the palette. The new palette will replace the previous one.

To copy a graphic or text block to a Library palette:

- Choose **Library palette** from the **Window** menu.

- Select the graphic or text block to place in the palette.

- Click on the + with the pointer tool.

- An Item information box may appear, as shown in Figure 9–7. Fill in the appropriate information. You may give the item a title, an author, a date, keywords to identify the object, and a description. If no information box appears, you can add this information by double-clicking on the object in the palette window. The dialog box will then appear.

- Click **OK.** If there are objects already in the palette, your object will be the last one on the list.

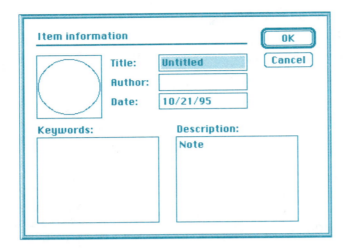

Figure 9–7
The Item information box lets you identify an object in several ways.

N O T E

To make it easier to find an object, the palette can be expanded by dragging the side or bottom margins in Windows or using the re-sizing box in Macintosh.

To copy a graphic or text block from a Library palette:

- Choose **Library palette** from the **Window** menu.

- Locate the object and drag it from the palette window to the publication. A loaded cursor will appear, as shown in Figure 9–8. When you release the mouse button, the object will appear.

Figure 9–8
Drag the loaded Library palette cursor to wherever you wish an object to appear and then click the cursor to unload it.

To search the Library palette for a particular object:

- Choose **Search library** from the **Options.**

- Search by keyword, name, or title by entering the appropriate information. You may search by combining two keywords using the Boolean options of *And*, *Or*, and *But Not* by clicking on the One keyword only box.

To close a Library palette:

- Click on the close box located in the upper-left corner of the palette.

1. Choose the **Library palette** from the Window menu. A palette named *Graphics* will appear. If it does not, **Open** the palette from **Options**. It will be located in your template file.

2. Use the options to create a new palette named **Lesson9.**

3. Copy the figure of the checkmark to the palette. Name it *Checkmark* if a dialog box appears. If a box does not appear, double-click on the figure to call up the box and then name it.

4. Open the palette named **Graphics.**

5. Search the palette by title for the graphic *Logo*.

6. Copy the figure labeled *Logo* to the farthest upper-left corner of the publication page. You may need to realign the figure once you have unloaded it. All parts should fit into the box formed by the upper and left margins and the column guides and the ruler guide.

EXERCISE 9–5

7. Close the Library palette.

8. Save the publication as **EX9-5.**

9. Leave the publication open for the next exercise.

USING THE COLOR PALETTE

Using color is a quick way to add interest to any publication. Although some businesses and schools do not have color printers or photocopiers, you may have that equipment available to you in the future.

Color can be assigned easily to text or to graphics created in PageMaker using the Color palette found in the Window menu.

To use the Color palette with existing text:

- Highlight the text to be assigned color using the text tool.
- Choose the **Color palette** from the **Window** menu.
- Choose the appropriate color.

To use the Color palette to create color text:

- Choose the **Color palette** from the **Window** menu.
- Select the text tool.
- Choose the appropriate color.
- Key in your text. The color chosen will be visible as your text appears.

To use the Color palette with an existing graphic:

- Choose the **Color palette** from the **Window** menu.
- Select the graphic with the pointer tool.
- **Both** is the default choice in the left-hand box above the color option. It refers to the outside line of the graphic as well as the fill color. To change both the fill to a color other than empty and the line color from black, click on a new color from the Color palette.
- To fill the graphic with a color without changing the line, change **Both** to **Fill** by clicking on the arrow beside **Line** and scrolling down to **Fill** (see Figure 9–9).

  -or-

  Click on the box icon to the right of the arrow.
- To change the line but not change the fill, change **Both** to **Line** by clicking on the arrow beside Line and scrolling down to Line (see Figure 9–9).

  -or-

  Click on the **line** icon to the right of the arrow.
- Click on the new color.

N O T E

If you assign color to graphics that you import into a publication, you will not be able to see the color on your screen; however, the graphic will print in that color on a Postscript printer.

Fill Box   Line Box

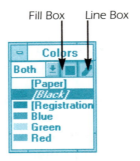

Figure 9–9
PageMaker gives you two ways to change the outside line of a graphic or the interior color: a pull-down menu and a diagonal line and a box graphic.

To create a color graphic with the Color palette:

- Choose the **Color palette** from the **Window** menu. Select a color.

- Choose either the **line, constrained-line, rectangle,** or **ellipse tool.**

- Draw the graphic. The line will be the selected color. The fill will be empty.

- Select **Line, Fill,** or **Both.**

- Choose the appropriate color.

EXERCISE 9–6

1. Choose the **Color palette.**

2. Highlight *Copper High School* in the logo.

3. Assign it the color blue.

4. Select the top line of the crossroads. Color it red.

5. Select the right vertical line. Color it blue.

6. Place the cursor to the right of the word *School.* Press **Return** or **Enter** twice.

7. Change the text color to red. Key in **"Where All Worlds Meet."** Include the quotation marks.

8. Draw a green line below the motto cutting through the two vertical lines.

9. Return to your page 1.

10. Save the publication as **EX9-6.**

11. Print the publication and end your PageMaker session.

TRUE/FALSE

In the blank space before each sentence, place a **T** if the statement is true and an **F** if it is false.

_____ 1. Your choice of Page setup determines the number of master pages.

_____ 2. The only rulers and guides you can use on a master page are column guides.

_____ 3. The Control palette is used with graphics, texts, and paragraphs.

_____ 4. Defining a style applies text attributes to individual words of text.

_____ 5. A Library palette stores frequently used graphics.

COMPLETION

Fill in the blank.

6. Explain how to number pages automatically.

   _____

7. List at least three attributes you can assign when defining styles.

   _____

   _____

8. Explain how the Control palette changes depending on the buttons you select.

   _____

   _____

9. What options do you have when searching in the Library palette?

   _____

   _____

10. When can't you assign color to a graphic?

   _____

   _____

R E V I E W

REVIEW EXERCISE 9–1

1. From the template directory *SHORTCUT*, open **MEMOFORM.**

2. In Page setup, change the number of pages to two double-sided pages but not facing. Click **OK.**

3. Select the right master page icon.

4. Copy the footer.

5. Select the left master page icon and paste the footer below the margin.

6. Create three columns on this page with .5 inch between them.

7. Place a horizontal ruler guide at the 1.5-inch mark. Add horizontal rulers at the 3-, 4-, 5-, 6-, 7-, and 8-inch marks.

8. Turn off Snap to guides. Lock guides.

9. Save the publication as **RE9-1** and leave it open for the next activity.

REVIEW EXERCISE 9–2

1. Return to the page 1 icon.

2. Key into a new text block **September 14.** Press Return or Enter three times. Key in **Immediately.**

3. Assign the style **Memo Text** to *September 14* and *Immediately.*

4. Align the text block so that it appears across from *Date:* and *Action Date:.*

5. Key into a new text block **Faculty and Staff.** Press Return or Enter three times. Key in **J. S. Potts.** Press Return or Enter three times. Key in **School Closings.**

6. Assign the style **Memo Text** to this text. Modify just this text to 18 points.

7. Align the text block so that *Faculty and Staff, J.S. Potts,* and *School Closings* appear below the titles *To, From,* and *Re.*

8. Define a new style. Title it **Memo Copy.** The style should be 10-point Times or Times Roman, left alignment, normal. It should be based on No style. Return to your page.

9. Place the text on the pasteboard onto the lower-right block below *Date:* and *Date Action:*. Make sure to display all text.

10. Assign the style **Memo Copy** to all the paragraphs of text.

11. Edit the style **Memo Copy.** Change it to 14-point with hyphenation off. Assign a Paragraph space of .2 inches After.

12. Assign the color red to the second paragraph of the text block. It begins with *It is important . . . .*

13. Save the publication as **RE9-2.**

14. Print page 1 of the publication and leave it open for the next activity.

REVIEW EXERCISE 9–3

1. Go to page 2.

2. Open the Library palette named *Tree*.

3. Copy the block labeled Primary 1 from the Library palette to the top of the left column below the first ruler guide. Center the object within the rectangle formed by the column guides and the ruler guides.

4. Copy Primary 2 to the top of the middle column. Copy Primary 3 to the top of the right column. Center each object and name within the rectangle formed by the column guides and the ruler guides.

5. Copy 1A into the rectangle below Primary 1. Center the box with the name within the rectangle.

6. Copy and center 1B, 1C, 1D, and 1E into the rectangles below 1A.

7. Copy and center 2A, 2B, 2C, 2D, and 2E below Primary 2. Copy and center 3A, 3B, 3C, 3D, and 3E below Primary 3.

8. Draw a red line between Primary 1 and Primary 2 and Primary 3.

9. Draw a blue line from Primary 1 down through 1A, 1B, 1C, 1D, and 1E. Do the same for Primary 2 and the boxes below it and Primary 3.

10. Save the publication as **RE9-3**.

11. Print page 2 of the publication and end your PageMaker session.

LESSON 10

Desktop Publishing Center

OBJECTIVES

After completing this lesson, you will be able to:

1. Create a logo.
2. Design a letterhead.
3. Plan a poster.
4. Set up a business card.
5. Design a certificate.
6. Plan an invitation.
7. Create a program.

Estimated Time: 2 hours

By working through the previous chapters of this book, you have developed PageMaker skills. In this chapter you will apply what you have learned to produce documents for a Desktop Publishing Center (DTP Center).

CREATING A LOGO

A logo is needed to identify DTP Center documents. A logo can combine text and graphics to represent a business name. A sample logo is shown in Figure 10–1.

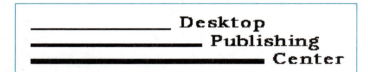

Figure 10–1
A logo can be an important way to identify an organization.

1. Create an original logo for the DTP Center. Include your school's name as part of the logo.

▶ **EXERCISE 10–1**

2. Copy the logo to the LOGOS Library palette. It will be necessary to drag a box around the logo with the pointer tool to select all the elements. Use your name to identify the logo in the palette.

3. Print the logo and close the publication.

DESIGNING A LETTERHEAD

A letterhead combines an organization's logo, name, address, telephone number, fax number, and Internet address to be used as stationery for business communication. A sample letterhead is shown in Figure 10–2.

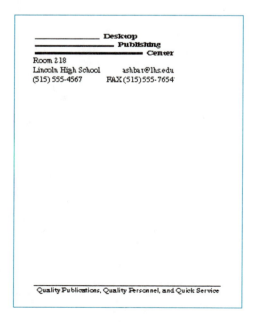

Figure 10–2
A letterhead can be designed in a variety of ways as long as the essential information is included. A slogan is frequently included.

1. Create an original letterhead for the DTP Center. Use the logo you created.

2. Save your work as **LTRHD**.

3. Print the letterhead and close the publication.

EXERCISE 10–2

PLANNING A POSTER

Posters are put up to announce information or events. It should be possible to read posters at a minimum distance of ten feet. When designing a poster, you need to include all the information necessary to convey your message. A sample poster is shown in Figure 10–3.

Figure 10–3
Graphics such as banners can make posters more appealing to the reader.

1. Create a poster using the following information:
   Senior High Banquet
   March 19 6:30 p.m.
   Elegant Steakhouse
   9701 Ave G.
   $9 a ticket
   Tickets go on sale January 10.

2. Save your work as **POSTER**.

3. Print the poster and close the publication.

EXERCISE 10–3

SETTING UP A BUSINESS CARD

Business cards are used to promote a business and the people who work in the business. A standard business card is 2 inches high and 3-1/2 inches wide, as shown in Figure 10–4. They usually include the following information:

Business logo
Business name

Names and job title(s) of one or more employees
Address of the business
Phone number of the business
Fax number of the business
Internet address

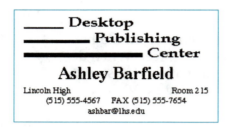

Figure 10–4
Many desktop publishing businesses produce business cards.

1. Design a business card for the DTP Center.

2. Save your work as **BUSCARD.**

3. Print the business card and close the publication.

▶ **EXERCISE 10–4**

DESIGNING A CERTIFICATE

Certificates, as shown in Figure 10–5, are used to recognize people for achievements. They usually include borders and contain the following information:

Purpose of certificate
Name of recipient
Date
Person awarding certificate

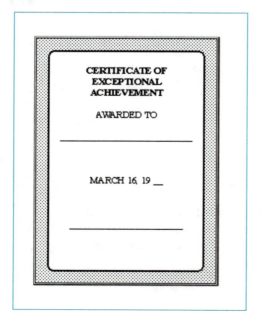

Figure 10–5
Certificates are important means of recognizing personnel.

1. Design a certificate for exceptional achievement. Include an interesting border.

EXERCISE 10–5

2. Save your work as **CERTIF.**

3. Print the certificate and close the publication.

PLANNING AN INVITATION

Creating a folded invitation like the one shown in Figure 10–6 requires you to rotate the information in one of the four quadrants 180 degrees. An invitation includes the following information:

Hosts of the event
Type of event
Location
Date
Time
RSVP

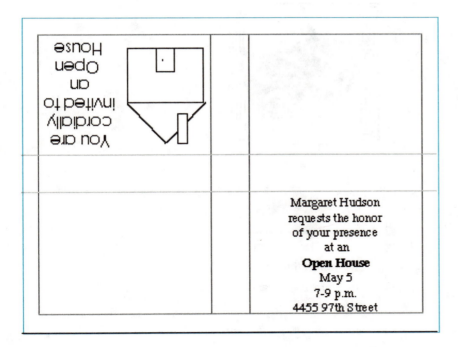

Figure 10–6
Printed invitations have become more common with the growth of desktop publishing.

1. Design an invitation. Use the drawing tools to create a graphic. Include the following information:

EXERCISE 10–6

Margaret Hudson
Open House
4455 97th Street
May 5
7–9 p.m.
no RSVP is needed

2. Save your work as **OPEN.**

3. Print the invitation and close the publication.

CREATING A PROGRAM

A program is usually a four-page document designed with inside facing pages (see Figure 10–7). The orientation is wide, with two columns per page. The column guide spacing should be twice the size of the outside margin.

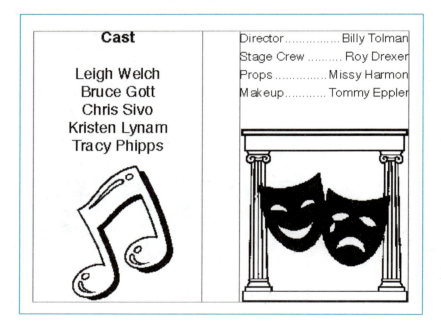

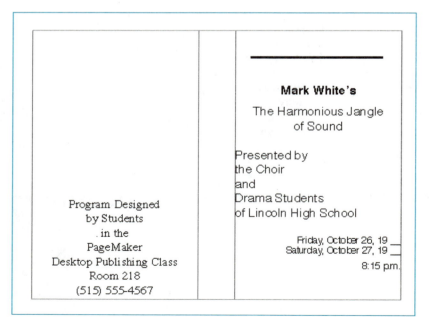

Figure 10–7

Programs can contain attractive graphics to recognize the event they are describing.

1. Design a program. It should contain the following information:

   Outside cover (page 1)
   Mark White's The Harmonious Jangle of Sound
   Presented by the Choir and Drama Students of Lincoln High School
   Friday, October 26, 19 __
   Saturday, October 27, 19 __
   8:15 p.m.

   Inside (page 2)
   Cast—Leigh Welch, Bruce Gott, Chris Sivo, Kristen Lynam, and Tracy Phipps

   Inside (page 3)
   Director—Billy Tolman
   Stage Crew—Roy Drexer
   Props—Missy Harmon
   Makeup—Tommy Eppler

   Outside (page 4)
   Program Designed by Students in the PageMaker Desktop Publishing Class
   Room 218
   (515) 555-4567

2. Save your work as **PROG.**
3. Print the program and close the publication.

DESKTOP PUBLISHING IN YOUR FUTURE

The simulation is over, and you are now an experienced desktop publisher. You can design documents like newsletters, brochures, programs, handbooks, business forms, and flyers to communicate messages effectively. These new skills will increase your ability to find jobs in the future. Organizations that use desktop publishing are diverse. They include government agencies, churches, newspapers, advertising agencies, colleges, volunteer services, publishing companies, and hospitals. Both small and large businesses use desktop publishing.

Whether you become a federal employee, a church secretary, a newspaper layout artist, an advertising executive, a college recruiter, a volunteer service director, a book publisher, or a publicity person for a hospital, your desktop publishing skills will be an asset. Good luck!

Index

5.0 icon, 2

scroll bar, 6
Search library option, 108
secondary margin
    guides for, 84-85
    for master pages, 100
selecting text blocks, 20
Send to back command, 56
serif typeface, 36
Set width command, 44
Shift key
    use in moving indent
        triangles, 89
    use in moving text block, 20
shortcuts, 99-113
    Color palette as, 109-110
    Control palette for, 101-102,
        105-107
    defining and applying styles
        with, 102-105
    keyboard, 4
    Library palette as, 107-109
    master pages as, 100-101
Show pasteboard command, 16
side margin, 84
Single pages, 100
single spaced text, 40
skewing objects, 68
slogan, 116
Snap to guides, 85-86
spacing, 40
    control palette and, 105
    Paragraph specifications
        dialog box and, 42
Spacing attributes dialog
    box, 43
special characters, 31-32
spell checker, 27-28
Spelling dialog box, 28
squares, drawing with rectangle
    tool, 51
Standoff measurement, 68
stationery, letterhead as, 116
story
    creating new, 27
    text as part of, 19
story editor, 25-34
    Control palette and, 101
    placing a new story created
        in, 27
    using, 26-27
    Utilities menu of, 27-32

Story menu
    Close story from, 26
    Display (from, 31
strikethru text, 37-38
Style option and palette, 103
styles, defining and applying,
    102-105
subdirectories, 7

T

tabloid-size pages, 75
tabs
    removing, 89
    repeat, 90
    setting, 89-91
    See also Indents/Tabs
tall orientation, 75
templates, sample
    publication, 7
text, 15-24
    advanced, 35-48
    Control palette and, 62
    copying, 17-18
    cutting, 17-18
    deleting, 17-18
    entering, 16-17
    highlighting, 17
    importing, 19
    Library palette and, 107
    moving, 18
    as an object, 72
    pasting, 17-18, 22
    placing graphics on, 19
    recurring, 100
    toolbox and, 5
    Type specifications dialog
        box and, 45
    vertical spacing of, 40
text blocks
    adding to master pages, 100
    changing size of, 20-22
    creating, 19-20
    deleting entire, 22
    editing story of existing, 26
    inline graphic as part of, 50
    manipulating, 22
    moving, 20
    pasting, 22
    selecting and deselecting, 20

    using handles to reflow
        columns within, 78
text margins, dotted lines
    indicate, 6
text style, keyboard shortcuts to
    change, 38
text tool, 5
    keying text with, 16-17
    pasting text with, 22
    selecting text with, 101-102
Text wrap option, 68-69
tick marks, 85
Times New Roman font, 37
title bar, 5
toggle function, 31, 86, 88
Toolbox, 5
    constrained-line tool
        from, 53
    drawing simple graphics
        with, 51
    ellipse tool from, 51-52
    line tool from, 53
    rectangle tool from, 51
    rotating tool on, 66
    text tool on, 16
Track command, 41-42
tracking
    changing with Control
        palette, 102
    selecting, 41-42
transforming objects, 63-68
triangles
    moving bottom, 89
    tab position, 89
type case, changing with
    Control palette, 102
typeface, 36-37. *See also* fonts
Type menu
    Alignment from, 40
    Font from, 36
    Indents/tabs option from,
    89-91
    Leading command
        from, 40-41
    Paragraph from, 42
    Paragraph specifications
        dialog box from, 92-93
    Set width from, 44
    Size from, 37
    Style option from, 103
    Track from, 42